Distance Tra

Arthur Lydiard/Garth Gilmour

Distance Training for Women Athletes

Meyer & Meyer Sport

British Library Cataloguing in Publication Data
A catalogue record for this book is available from the British Library

Lydiard / Gilmour :
Distance Training for Women Athletes / Arthur Lydiard; Garth Gilmour.
– Oxford : Meyer & Meyer Sport (UK) Ltd., 1999
ISBN 1-84126-002-9

© 1999 by Meyer & Meyer Sport (UK) Ltd.
Oxford, Aachen, Olten (CH), Vienna,
Québec, Lansing/ Michigan, Adelaide, Auckland, Johannesburg
e-mail: verlag@meyer-meyer-sports.com
Cover design: Birgit Engelen, Stolberg
Cover Photo: Sportpressefoto Bongarts, Hamburg
Photos inside by Arthur Lydiard
Editorial: Dr. Irmgard Jaeger, Aachen; John Coghlan
Cover and Type exposure: frw, Reiner Wahlen, Aachen
Typesetting: Quai
Printed and bound in Germany by Druckpunkt, Offset GmbH, Bergheim
ISBN 1-84126-002-9

CONTENTS

Foreword 7

1. Amazing but not Amazons 9

2. Why Run? 13

3. The Physiological Factor 17

4. And the Psychology 21

5. Women of all Ages Can Run 23

6. Elite Runners 25

7. Health Aspects 29

8. Running as Recreation 31

9. The Technique of Running 35

10. The Path to Full Potential 37

11. The Competitive Athlete 41

12. Fitting in with the Family 45

13. Equipment – Especially Shoes 49

14. Diet 53

15. Vitamins and Minerals 57

16. Changes to the Body 63

17. Injury Avoidance and Treatment 65

18. Setting out Your Schedule 71

19. The Schedules 81

20. Postscript – The Legend Strides on 119

Foreword

In the never-ending war of the sexes, the women will probably never win, but they have won ground in some significant battles. One of those battle arenas is distance running, in which the improvement shown by women in the short time they have applied themselves has easily outpaced the progress of male runners.

Their opportunities have been limited to only the past two decades because officialdom was stubbornly reluctant to promote or even allow women's middle and distance events, even when the evidence was there that they could not only come to no harm but they could perform outstandingly if they pursued correct training programmes.

Finally, a 3,000-metres race for women was included in the Olympic Games and the dam of resistance burst. Within a short time the fairer and wrongly-termed weaker sex convincingly demonstrated their ability to run even marathons aggressively and successfully.

But, only 25 years ago, Arthur Lydiard watched a schoolgirls' 800-metres race in Auckland, New Zealand, which was open to all ages from 13 to 19. No other middle distances race was provided for the 13-year-old girls, so, if they were not fast enough for shorter events and they wanted to compete, they were forced to run against much more mature girls – and the difference in the physical development of young women between 13 and 19 is significant. One 13-year-old collapsed after the first lap because trying to match the pace set by the older girls was far beyond her ability.

Lydiard bluntly told a teacher who was on the committee which planned the programme that she was responsible for the girl's collapse because the programme was totally unrealistic; and he was pleased to note that, in the following years, middle distance races were programmed for the various age-groups.

Lydiard forcefully promoted longer races, such as 3,000 metres, for all secondary school ages. How else, he argued, were the younger and slower ones who could not foot it in sprint events, to be encouraged to train for and participate in a sport that could only do them a great deal of good? Among those who were not natural sprinters could well be youngsters with the latent talent to become champions.

Now, of course, women all around the world are producing fine middle and distance performances, because they now approach their training exactly as men do, and run up to 200 kilometres a week.

In a book we wrote in 1978, Lydiard and I noted that women were already running the marathon in times under 2:40, and he predicted then that they would soon get under 2:30. The first woman broke that barrier only two years later.

Today, Lydiard predicts that 2:20 will be the benchmark regularly broken by women marathoners.

This book is designed to help them to do it and to excel in all other distances. For women competing in other sports, this book provides essential guidelines for establishing the base of speed and endurance on which to build the specific skills of their chosen sport, whether swimming or rowing, ball games, field events or triathlons, orienteering or skiing, or the host of other activities that now attract women into competition or simple recreation for fitness.

Garth Gilmour
Auckland, New Zealand
November 1998

1 Amazing but not Amazons

When women began running long distances, the talk centred quite often on the likelihood that they would all become fierce-looking Amazons. This was both a myth and physiologically wrong. Experience since has proved that women do not become masculine and bulkily-muscled through running. Men do not so why should it be expected that women would?

Many of the world's best women athletes are extremely feminine and attractive, even though they train like men and perform at the highest levels. Physique is the basic form and structure of the body, compounded of bone, muscle and fat. The female can never develop muscles as strong as the male, so resistance and strength training will never produce male-like firmness of muscles nor increase muscle size to the same extent. Muscle fibre cannot be increased so women have little to fear.

In fact, the inherent anatomical attributes of the female enable her to excel in sports without any tendency to masculinity, or a predominance of male characteristics. She will excel because she is endowed with a body which enables her to perform with greater skill, if with less sheer strength.

In the great testing ground of the marathon the woman is at some advantage because she has a greater natural proportion of muscle fat than the man, which enables her to draw out her reserves far more efficiently. It is a factor which eliminates that dreaded 'wall' that so many male runners hit at 32 kilometres or so, when body reserves run out and the oxygen debt begins to build. Women certainly seem to finish in an apparently fresher state than men and, in race times, they are rapidly getting nearer the front in increasing numbers.

Many fallacies surround the influence of exercise and sports participation on menstruation. It has been generally accepted that women should avoid vigorous activity immediately before, during and immediately after their period; but it is a general conclusion not based on fact. Menstruation is a biological phenomenon which places a particular burden on the blood production system, so it was assumed that any additional physical stress on the organism during this time would overload to some extent the physiological function and disturb the cycle in some harmful way.

Changes do take place but it has been established that those changes vary between individuals and range from beneficial to harmful. In other words, it is entirely an individual matter; activity which upsets one woman will not necessarily upset another. Research suggests that vigorous activity, even to the point of voluntary fatigue, will benefit as many as it will harm in terms of the length and volume of menstrual flow.

It is now accepted that the direction of the changes is related to the mental and physical characteristics, and status of the individual female, so that the restriction of physical activity during menstruation should be a generally applied principle but one applied with discretion, and with regard to each individual case.

Anyone who measures up to these general requirements should not need to limit activity during menstruation:

- Enjoys good health.
- Is physically fit and in condition to do the specific activity.
- Does not perform exercises that require excessive abdominal contractions and compression or cause excessive shock to or bouncing of the organism.
- Does not perform activities that require explosive action, such as the shot put and discus.
- Avoids extreme cold and heat.
- Is not compelled or coerced into participation against her will.

Equally, modern biological and medical evidence indicates that the female benefits during pregnancy, and in the post-parturition period, from competitive sports and exercise.

The female, in addition to a lighter and weaker build with less muscle bulk, which makes her generally about one-third less strong than the male in either individual muscle or total strength capacity, also has a cardio-pulmonary reserve capacity about two-thirds of the male. She is therefore unable to obtain the same maximal oxygen intake, ventilation volume and cardiac output, as the male during physical performance.

Her loosely constructed abdominal organs, the inclined pelvis, producing a greater abdominal area, and the pelvic floor constitute weaknesses in her physique but, in spite of this, she has the qualities and the physiological capacities to enable her to perform the same types of movements, and engage in the same physical activities, as the male. She is limited only by intensity and strength. At her own level she can match the male in activities requiring speed, strength, endurance and skill.

When I first trained men in their teens I was cautious about the amount of training I could give them. I knew what a man could stand but I was uncertain what a youth could take without impairing his performance. I eventually concluded that boys could run up to 160 kilometres a week, as long as the speed was controlled to an economic level, and that they could also absorb an equal mileage in supplementary jogging.

I now know that women, and young girls, at their own level, can train just as long as men. To begin they should jog daily on grass – parks and golf courses are ideal – to tone muscles comfortably while the respiratory and circulatory systems are being conditioned. Fifteen minutes a day is enough to begin with, but, once any initial soreness has disappeared from the muscles, the running should be increased to provide a longer run every second or third day. All daily times can then be extended as long as the balance is maintained between long runs and alternating short runs to allow for recovery. Without recovery there will be no improvement.

This is easier than it may seem because the body's reaction to this training regime is a spectacularly rapid improvement in stamina and general condition.

Cross-country training and races can then be brought into the system before the runner progresses to a conditioning schedule, resistance training and track and speed work, which place more demands on the body's resources, and depend for success on the quick recovery which only adequate stamina and strong condition give.

Schedules follow later in this book but a typical marathon-type training programme would be something like this:

Monday:	One hour's steady running.
Tuesday:	Half-hour fartlek (explained below).
Wednesday:	One and a half hours' steady running.
Thursday:	One hour's steady running.
Friday:	Half-hour fartlek.
Saturday:	One and a half hours' steady running.
Sunday:	One hour's steady running.

The fartlek, or speed play, should include more stride-outs than sprints. During the half-hour, mostly run at an even pace, stride out periodically for any distance up to 200 metres, occasionally increase speed on uphill slopes and stride out easily on downhill slopes, provided they are not too steep.

The aim is to finish all training sessions feeling comfortably tired, that you could do more. Run to my motto: TRAIN DO NOT STRAIN.

2 Why Run?

Let's get one thing clear first. Running is not exactly jogging but there can be little distinction between the two. When you begin running your speed may approximate the pace of a jogger; and so can the pace of a runner when she is moving along easily. Others may classify the slower, six or eight minute mile as a jog, but it depends precisely on what the particular runner is doing with her running programme.

Ultra-distance runners – an exclusive group largely dominated in recent years by women and, notably, by the world champion New Zealander Sandra Barwick – may take twelve minutes to cover a mile but, when those miles are strung together for hours and even days on end, that's running far beyond the average person's capability.

Europe's many 100-kilometres runs frequently see women recording better average times than many men. An example: Hamburg's Eva Westphal ran 100 kilometres in 10 hours 11 minutes when she was 53. She beat men who could run 10,000 metres in 36-38 minutes, compared with her 42-43 minutes. American Natalie Cullimore ran 161 kilometres in 18 hours, nearly two hours slower than her best, and finished ahead of all the men.

It is an interesting fact that women are more likely to suffer far less than men in the closing stages of a marathon, and also tend to run more even splits, or even better second halves than first halves. This is serious racing by serious athletes.

Equally, the woman who makes a commitment to running regularly just for her own personal fitness is serious about what she is doing, even if she has no intention of ever competing. Whatever the goal, the activity of achieving it is a serious undertaking.

Why run? The reasons are many and varied. For the companionship of running with other women; to strive for competitive targets from short races to marathons and beyond; to bid to become a world champion, which could also be referred to as self-exploration, the quest to find how good you are, how better you could be; to gain and maintain a level of fitness to help you to work better, sleep better, run a home and family better; to stay in tune with other family members who run, jog or race; just for the sheer pleasure of being fit, out in the fresh air, feeling great. That can also be classified as self-esteem.

A schedule of running to build physical endurance, enhanced lung and heart capacity, a trimmer, stronger body and a keener, more agile mind leads to any or all of these objectives. What you do is an individual choice, but how you do it is governed by immutable rules. There are no shortcuts.

My system of conditioning was developed half a century ago during years of experimentation, mainly with my own body, and proved beyond question with years of total dominance of middle and distance running, first in New Zealand and then throughout the world. It has produced Olympic Games champions and record holders, world champions and record setters, and has been unchallenged by any other training system. The long-distance endurance running method I developed has been adopted all around the world by athletes and coaches; some have amended it and fiddled with the finer points but none has improved on it.

It also formed the basis of the world-wide jogging movement, which we launched in New Zealand three decades ago after I had taught a group of male heart patients to run themselves back to fitness – so successfully that some of them competed in marathons. Untold numbers of people who took up jogging became so fit and enthusiastic they have formed the bulk of fields in marathon races ever since.

These included men and women who had not moved above walking pace since they gave up youthful sporting activities, and at first could not jog more than a few hundred yards. Some could not even manage that but, with controlled programmes, training without straining, they achieved phenomenal gains in a matter of months.

Anyone can do it. You can do it.

In 1980, in her book, *Running Free,* world-class marathoner and author Joan Ullyot, to whom we are indebted for some of the philosophies in this book, wrote:

"My distinction between jogging and running is based on motivation rather than speed. To me, a jogger is concerned primarily with her health, her figure or her appearance. She may not like the activity at all but feels it is good for her, or a duty. The runner, by contrast, likes to run. The sport is enjoyable in itself, leads to a warm glow, a sense of relaxation and contentment. Whether she moves along at 12 minutes-mile, or 8, whether she runs in the Olympic Games, or just down the rural road to the letterbox, the woman who loves to run is a runner.

"By this definition, most of us started out as joggers. We didn't see runners pound past us in a road race, eyes slightly glazed, mouths open, obviously straining to win, and think to ourselves, 'Gee, that looks like a lot of fun, I think I'll try it.' I remember my own reaction when I inadvertently saw the Boston marathon leaders flash past me ten years ago. I thought, 'Why would grown men run through the streets of Boston in their underwear, obviously inflicting pain on themselves?' I shuddered with distaste and turned away. The runner's mentality was a mystery to me. I wasn't even a jogger yet – I had a pre-jogger's scorn of road runners."

Joan Ullyot, a Harvard graduate and specialist in sports medicine and physical fitness counselling, mother of two sons and now 58, subsequently overcame her revulsion to become a national and international distance running celebrity and the only woman who is an acknowledged guru of the running world.

She did it.

3 The Physiological Factor

In 1924, when Johnny Weismuller, later famed for his Tarzan films, won the 400-metres freestyle swimming in 5.04 at the Paris Olympics, he was so exhausted he had to be rescued before he drowned. In 1968, Debbie Meyer, who was 15, won the women's 400-metres freestyle in 4.31 at the Mexico Olympics, and the 800 metres in 9.24, a time which a decade earlier a handful of male swimmers struggled to equal. The result? A telling demonstration that the brute muscle strength of Weismuller was no match for the endurance and technique which propelled little Debbie Meyer to her gold medals.

Discussing this some years ago, the superb German physician and sports coach, Ernst Van Aaken, said it proved what many sports experts refused to acknowledge: That woman, because of her physical and psychic constitution, is an endurance performer as long as the stresses imposed on her do not involve excessive muscle-strength demands. At the time he wrote this, others were dismissing this fact by comparing males to females in cycle ergometer tests, hand-strength tests and similar procedures. They were establishing that men had muscle strength and women dit not, which was true but totally devalued female performance capacity in all respects.

At that time the absolute best endurance performance in swimming that Van Aaken knew of was produced by Jenny Kammersgaad, of Denmark, who covered 90 kilometres. Since then, of course, women have featured alongside men in some remarkable endurance swims under conditions which tested not only their endurance but also their courage and tenacity. It is almost certain that they are less likely to give up than men when the conditions become aggravated.

Van Aaken recalled that, in the early 1950s, not long ago in terms of male athletic history, arguments raged around the 800-metres distance for women, which he was advocating in Europe. He was castigated when he argued that not only could women run the distance but it was still far too short of what they could excel at. One newspaper writer suggested that stretchers, ambulances and doctors should be posted at the finish line of the 1954 German national 800-metres race for women, ready to rush the mortally exhausted women to the nearest hospital.

Certainly, it was known that some women did collapse after running the distance but only because they had made no effort to condition themselves properly to run it competitively and drove themselves into oxygen debt long before the end of their races. Incidentally, the same critical journalist subsequently, in a complete about-face, reported after the preliminary heats: "It was a wonderful image of grace and beauty to see Marianne Weiss fly easily towards the finish during her final sprint."

Another 15 years passed before the German Federation decided it was safe to add the 1,500 metres and longer races to their programmes.

What was ignored then, as it is still sometimes overlooked today, is that youngsters in the 8 to 12 age-group can play for hours on end without tiring, and that girls of the same age are often superior to boys of that age because of their thinner bodies and lower weight. Children, without thinking what they are doing, will stop playing when they feel tired, recover quickly and continue to play as long as the sun still shines, and usually until they are called in for a meal.

I consider it is quite safe, and even beneficial, to move girls and boys as young as six or seven into running programmes which involve long distances without producing any undesirable effects. Under the age of 15 youngsters can handle a great deal of aerobic training because their capacity to use oxygen in relation to body weight is greater than an adult's. But too much anaerobic training should be avoided because of their highly sensitive nervous systems.

Competitive racing over sprints up to 200 metres, or middle and distance races from 800 metres upwards, cannot harm youngsters. The danger distances are races over 300 or 400 metres because these involve sustained speed running which can incur oxygen debts greater than young systems can handle. They can be sick, black out or suffer other distress. They can run 200 metres quite fast but the next 100 or 200 metres could bring them to exhaustion at the point in the race when the greatest effort to win is required.

Youngsters recognise 800 metres events as non-sprints and will settle into a pace they can manage without abnormal distress.

In New Zealand, girls and boys run cross-country from an early age – over 3000 to 5,000 metres from the age of eight – and it is a fascinating insight into their capabilities that, though they may seem to have run themselves fairly well out by the finish, within minutes they will be up and playing games.

Sustained running will cause no damage. Sustained speed will. That is the difference in emphasis which has wrecked many potential champions in countries all over the world.

Gundar Haegg's coach, Homar, who knew his running, said: "If you can get a boy in his teens and encourage him to train and not race until he is matured, then you have laid the foundations of an Olympic champion." This is equally true of girls and young women.

Statistics going back more than a century prove that women are more enduring than men. Consider the difference in life expectancy. Women, on average, live much longer than men, and the gap is tending to widen in many countries.

Some 40 per cent of a man's body is muscle, compared with about 23 per cent for women. But women have more subcutaneous fat than men and thus have better energy reserves and protection from cold. A simple matter of fat metabolism but it gives women an advantage that a lot of good male distance runners might die for.

About the only problem some women have is that they get so wide in the hips that they can no longer bring their legs through as fast as the slimmer-hipped women. But this does not stop wide-hipped women from producing exceptional times and performances because the disadvantage can be counterbalanced by the proper conditioning and running technique for their specific build.

As I have said, women have brought their marathon best times down to 2:20, and I see no reason why they cannot keep moving below that mark. A lot depends on where marathons are run of course. Some marathon routes will never produce world's fastest times because of the nature of the terrain and the weather conditions to which runners are exposed. But the Dutch marathon traditionally sees some of the fastest times clocked up because it is flat, and the conditions are almost always calm. The runner who hits those conditions at the right state of preparedness can almost guarantee a personal best.

4 And the Psychology

The one muscle with which men and women can train equally is the heart. The skeletal muscles of women work slowly and with endurance, like heart muscle tissue, whereas men's muscles generally are more suited to explosive functions, as in sprinting and shorter races out to 800 metres. Men burn more carbohydrates during exercise while women seem to use a relatively higher amount of fatty acids and, possibly, cholesterol.

As Van Aaken expressed it: "Psychologically, men are often more explosive, inconstant, not enduring and in pain and exertion – especially among high performance athletes – somewhat snivelling. Woman is the opposite: tough, constant, enduring, level and calm under endurance exertion and in the pain to which her biology exposes her (child-bearing). On the average, she is more patient than man. Armed with these advantages, women are in a position to do endurance feats previously considered impossible."

He formed that opinion some 50 years ago, and it has been corroborated ever since by the dramatic achievements of women in the tough fields of distance running, triathlons, duathlons, cross-country skiing and mountain biking.

About that time Miki Gorman, who weighed only 38 kg, said after winning the 1974 Boston marathon in 2:47: "I can't run much faster but I can run much, much farther."

New Zealander Sandra Barwick, who performed brilliantly in races up to 1,000 miles long, is a latter-day example of woman's incredible endurance. She was first woman home in the Sri Chinmoy IAU World Championship over that distance in New York in 1988, a distance never before achieved by a woman; first woman and second finisher in the same race in 1991 —when the distance was 1,300 miles (2,092 kilometres); running world records for 48 hours, 6 days, 700 miles, 1,000 kilometres, 1,500 kilometres, 2,000 kilometres and 1,300 miles to demonstrate the consistency with which she could grind out the distance hour after hour and day after day in spite of extreme agony from blistered, swollen and bleeding feet and legs and other physical distress.

And she exemplified her womanliness in all her races. She always paused short of the finishing line in any road or track ultrathon she raced to change into fresh running gear, do her hair and apply make-up. And she was always smiling. The pain she often suffered was never allowed to show.

In 1992, to mark and raise money for Diabetes Awareness Week, she ran 2,000 kilometres from one end of New Zealand to the other. Towards the end of the run she reached a central North Island city, Rotorua, in time to take part in the annual marathon round Rotorua's lake, one of the toughest marathon courses in the world. She finished that event in 3:54, feeling "absolutely great all the way" and leaving her male support runners behind, and then continued on her run northwards.

Barwick was ultra-looks conscious too, almost to vanity, and she was far from the general concept of long-distance runners. The University of Auckland Sports Performance Unit said after testing her: "The somatotype (body shape) is untypical of a long-distance runner, exhibiting a tendency towards muscularity rather than the lean bean-stick figure." Her maximum oxygen uptake was far superior to values seen in other women of her age – then 43 – and not significantly far behind the world's elite women athletes, but the researchers were startled by how average a person Barwick proved to be.

The unit's chief, Steve Hollings, a former international athlete and Olympic Games team official, who saw her run 1,000 miles in New York in 14 days with no real medical support, no five-star accommodation, sleeping in tents, eating indifferent food, with poor sanitation, generally marginal conditions, little recognition, no financial rewards, suffering pain and shocking conditions in rain, cold and wind, classed her and two team-mates, Jos Smith and Max Marsh, as "the three most remarkable people I have met".

Hollings said that any other elite athlete would have walked away in half an hour from competing on those terms.

Significantly, two of the three were women. Quite average women who demonstrated that, if the will is there, anyone can do it.

For many years, once women began to be admitted to long-distance running events, they had to contend with an additional handicap – the men they were running against. Many of them resented the presence of women, particularly those women they could not match strides with, but the animosity slowly gave way to admiration, however grudging. Those pioneering women were tough in mind as well as body. They had to be to overcome the macho hostility, and they smoothed the path for the tens of thousands who have since followed them into the pleasures, the exhilaration, the satisfaction of running distance on an equal footing with men, with equal recognition of their rightful place in this sporting arena.

5 Women of all Ages Can Run

I have already suggested that females can begin regular running over substantial distances from the age of six or seven. They can begin running at any age from then on, provided they first tell their doctors what they intend doing and get a medical clearance before going ahead. Old age is no more a barrier than childhood to the enjoyment of sensible, controlled running.

New Zealander Ailsa Forbes became a celebrity in her own country when she launched into a running career in her sixties, and became a consistent performer in veterans' competitions. She was almost always the oldest in the field, often the only entrant in her age-group and usually last to finish, but she did everything with an infectious cheerfulness and an endearingly dogged determination. Finding running gave her a whole new lease of life and a whole new circle of friends and companions.

The joggers' clubs which sprang up around New Zealand in the 60s as people picked up on my message of running for fun and fitness began as almost exclusively male domains, but women gradually filtered in and today form a significantly large proportion of the organised jogging movement. They come along at all ages, in all shapes and sizes but with one common factor: their pleasure in finding a whole new wellspring of fitness and well-being.

The important elements for any women deciding to go running are patience and self-control. There is no need to become competitive, unless that appeals as fitness develops, and there should be no aspect of competitiveness during the conditioning stages. If you run with companions do not race them, or be tempted by them into finishing sprints or other demonstrations of rivalry.

And, if the urge develops to test yourself against the rest of the world, discipline and patience become even more important. I have often said, and still say, that the transition from non-runner to accomplished performer, or from average runner to champion, takes up to four years because that is how long it takes to build the foundation of stamina and endurance on which successful competitive running depends. You can follow shortcuts, but the results of shortcuts are, inevitably, short-lived.

6 Elite Runners

In my coaching days I did not deal much with elite women runners, apart from Heather Thompson (nee Matthews), but I took a great many high school girls, teenagers, to international successes they had never imagined they could attain. My lack of work with top-class women is not entirely surprising – the first mile race for women was not run until 1958, and they found it a great deal easier to run than to get permission to stage the event.

One of the first competitors, Robin Hames, explained years later: "We had to battle to get longer races for women in the 1950s. It was not enough just to be athletes. We had to become club officials and then get elected as centre delegates, and then we had to put our case to New Zealand Amateur Athletic Association meetings that were nearly all men. We were battered from all sides. They just weren't 'buying' that women could run anything over 220 yards."

This sounds ridiculous in today's scene, and was made obviously ridiculous very quickly when, in 1962, Marise Chamberlain broke five minutes in her first mile, and smashed the world's record in her second at 4:41.4, including a world best 1,500 metres of 4:19.0 on the way.

Matthews had been an exceptional teenage athlete but had lost confidence and direction. Very quickly she regained composure and strength, and she and several other women became dominant forces in New Zealand and international women's middle distance events through to the early 70s. She was a veteran when, in the 1978 Commonwealth Games 3,000 metres, she faced runners with times up to 15 seconds faster than her best, including the Commonwealth record holder. She showed the courage and daring that distinguished many of my runners, such as Murray Halberg and Peter Snell, both 1960 Olympic gold medalists, by racing to the lead in the final lap and holding out all but one of the field. She went on to build a world reputation, particularly in veterans' events. At 32 she ran 3,000 metres in 9:12; at 41 she ran 3,000 metres in 9:16.

The great New Zealand sports writer and statistician, Peter Heidenstrom, in his New Zealand classic, *Athletes of the Century*, ranked her second behind Anne Audain, a world record holder and outstanding road racer, in his all-time 3,000 metres list.

Among my troupe of young women Heather Carmichael won the New Zealand high schools 1,500 metres and cross-country championships and, when she was 18 in 1978, won the Peach Tree Road Race, and ran third in the United States cross-country championships. Her blooming career came to an end when she slipped down some stairs and injured her back.

I arranged a United States college scholarship for another girl, Christine McMeeken. Two years later she was the American cross-country champion and went on to finish seventh overall in the World Cross-country Championship. Christine was an avid trainer, she loved running miles, and it paid off as we had predicted.

All my girls, who ranged from 15 to 19 years of age, ran big mileages. I went out with them for an hour and a half twice a week, and they did substantial weekend mileages and subsidiary jogging miles.

At that time they held every secondary school middle distance, distance and cross-country championship in New Zealand, dominating their races just as my male runners, including Snell, Halberg, Olympic medalist Barry Magee, Bill Baillie and others, held all the men's national titles from the half-mile to the marathon for a number of years. And, like the men, they were developed from quite ordinary beginnings. The point here is that you do not need to have superman or superwoman qualities, or any exceptional gifts, to become elite athletes; all you need is the will to progress and the right conditioning and training schedule to go with it.

And there is no reason why women cannot train as hard as men, as long as they keep within their own limitations. It is a question of listening to your own body. If it is telling you to ease off, ease off. If it tells you halfway through a scheduled training session that it had enough, stop. If you do not force it your body will come back stronger than ever.

Joan Ullyot recorded the facts from a study in the United States which compared elite athletes with good and untrained runners to see exactly how they differed. The researchers could find no physiological characteristics which reliably distinguished between elite and good runners, who were drawn from a local university running team. They were all lean and fit. Matched against an equally lean collection of sedentary students, most of the physiological differences simply determined that all the runners were fit and the non-runners were not.

Between the good and the elite groups a few measurements indicated the elite were the fitter – their average resting pulse was 47.1 compared with 52.4 and maximal oxygen consumption was 76.9 against 69.2. This was hardly dramatic but the untrained figures were – 65.0 pulse and 54.2 oxygen consumption.

The body fat comparisons were 4.7 per cent elite, 6.1 per cent good and 8.2 per cent untrained. This is interesting but not particularly enlightening. Probably the real difference is that the elite runners trained harder than the merely good; in fact they averaged 136 km a week and the good only 96 km a week.

What threw rational conclusions into disarray was the discovery that Steve Prefontaine, at that time holder of ten American distance records, had an oxygen consumption of 84.4 but that year's outstanding athlete, Olympian Frank Shorter, who had beaten nearly all the others in the elite group, came in at 71.3.

Excellence, it was concluded, remains a physiological mystery. Joan Ullyot's conclusion was that it was about 5 per cent physical and 95 per cent mental – a matter of drive, willpower and attitude rather than any physical endowment.

That is something that will show in a race. Runner A, no better than runner B, suddenly shoots past B with apparent ease, perhaps even with an encouraging comment to B. B will either respond and go with A or be reduced to a jelly of despair and defeatism. Perhaps it is a matter of determining mentally to look and act better than you feel with the aim of demoralising your rivals. Perhaps that is a secret weapon that distinguishes the elite from the merely good.

Women athletes, perhaps unwittingly, can have this effect on their male opponents in long-distance races. Watch the reaction of a bunch of males, plugging along at what they consider a good pace, when a mere woman cruises up from behind and goes past. Men who are not yet prepared to accept that women are better equipped than they are for endurance running, and are now able and prepared to put in the training mileages to perfect that edge, can go to pieces at that point.

7 Health Aspects

Quoting Ernst Van Aaken again: "For health and its cultivation, a person needs two legs and a path for walking and running."

As simple as that and a most succinct case for going running to get fit. Quite apart from its comparative cheapness compared with many other sporting activities, it can be enjoyed anywhere anytime. And it becomes critical quite early, because the teenager, unless she exercises, is a prey to weight gain and the weight is always fat.

Fat contains hydrogen which cannot be burned off by the fat person or the untrained body because the oxygen needed to chemically change the hydrogen to water and energy just is not there. Some 2,000 litres of oxygen are needed to burn one kilogram of body fat – figure that out for a person with many kilograms overweight when it is established that only two or three litres of oxygen a minute are assimilated from 50 to 60 litres of air during light endurance running. In short, if fat is allowed to accumulate, it will have a tendency to hang around a long time.

So, how do we latch onto that extra oxygen? We can take long walks, climb a mountain, ride a bicycle, go cross-country skiing – the finest conditioning exercise of all – or we can simply tie on a pair of comfortable running shoes, step outside the door and go running. And if we run long enough and regularly enough, the fat will go.

But while it may be simple, it is not necessarily easy. The best things in life rarely are. You will have to condition yourself to be able to run comfortably for up to 45 minutes before the fat meltdown really begins. Up to then you will perspire a lot and seem to be losing weight, but the loss will be only water which will be quickly replaced.

But, meantime, all the extra oxygen you are taking in will be doing good things for your lungs, your heart, your brain and other organs. Remember that you can survive a long time without eating but only a few seconds without oxygen will induce unconsciousness, and five minutes means death. Unlike food, you cannot see it but nothing is more vital.

So, forgetting the fat issue, a daily half-hour run will deliver enough oxygen to give protection from coronary problems, circulatory upsets and probably other disorders which threaten the human organism.

I am not, and have never been, a diet freak. One woman's food could be another woman's poison; food likes and dislikes can be so powerful that one person could not comfortably digest, let alone swallow, food that another thoroughly enjoys. We discuss this aspect of health in a later chapter.

8 Running as Recreation

When you decide you want to get into an activity or sport which will help you to get more out of life, your first target has to be to achieve a state of fitness in which you can enjoy whatever it is you want to do. The beginner's first steps should be to see her doctor for a medical examination which will show whether you should or should not take up the activity. Even young people have died in fun runs from unsuspected and undetected sources. The risk of adding to that number is not worth taking.

Today's doctors recognise the value of restrained exercise and understand its benefits. So, get medical approval before you get going.

Running or jogging is the perfect conditioner for all sports because it is the most convenient builder of stamina, so it is important now to understand how to go about it sensibly so that you do not upset your metabolism, and how to run correctly so that you do not waste energy or risk injuries.

If you are a big woman beginning to learn the joy of running, your initial slowness means you will be hitting the ground hard. The faster you run the lighter you hit, but fast running is a measured time away for the novice. You will begin like all runners – landing almost flat-footed on the outside of the foot and then rolling through onto the ball of the foot for, ideally, a push off with the toes. So the correct shoes are vital and that is another subject for later discussion.

Observe a sprinter and you will see that, at speed, she does not run heel and toe; her centre of gravity is carried well forward so that she lands on the ball of the feet and drives immediately off the toes.

The chance, therefore, is that the heavier beginner-runner will experience some initial jarring and thumping. Unless the feet are properly shod that could lead to trouble in the joints.

Incidentally, cycling is a good alternative exercise for cardiac development and general fitness if running does not suit. So, too, is rowing because of its leg-arm action. Swimming is beneficial but not as effective because body weight is supported against gravity in the water.

Whatever you choose to do, the main requirement is to keep the activity within strict limits. If you run with others, suppress the competitive instinct; running for health and fitness is not a race, nor is systematic training for an athletic career. Save the competition for the events you compete in.

Cardiac development is a progression which lasts for several years, perhaps the rest of your life, but only if you do not thrash yourself at the outset. Seek advice if you can. Even champions like to help other people along the road they have followed. Coaches have vast knowledge which can be tapped.

Let's begin. Jog out for five minutes, turn and jog back – but do not make the mistake of finishing with a sprint. That is harmful. If you make it back in the same time, you have already learnt to move aerobically. If you struggle home, you've gone out too fast for your condition. Spend a few days balancing this ten-minute run to accustom leg, arm and body muscles to the exercise.

Then begin adding time on your feet. When you can do 15 minutes every day, or at least every other day, step up to a run of 30 minutes, followed by two days at 15 minutes, another of 30 minutes, two of 15 minutes and so on. Always give your body time for adequate recovery. Gradually step up to 45-minute runs, separated by two of 15 minutes, and then an hour-long run plus two of 15 minutes. Go about it patiently and comfortably and you will be astonished at how quickly you reach this pinnacle.

Now you can extend as long as you feel. It may seem faster progress to run 15 minutes a day every day, then 30 minutes a day, then 45 a day, but it will not have the same effect on your metabolism, and will take you three times as long to achieve the goals my method achieves. You must not neglect those recovery days – they are essential.

This method was used for the world's first jogging group, who were about 20 businessmen in Auckland, New Zealand. Most had had mild heart attacks and were aged from 40 up to 70-plus. Within eight months eight of them ran a full marathon which, considering they could not manage 100 metres at the start, was a remarkable demonstration of the values of the systematic and patient approach. One 74-year-old who had had several heart attacks ran 20 miles (32 kilometres) without stopping inside six months. He also shed about 60 lb (27 kg) in weight. A 47-year-old with no previous experience also shed that kind of weight, and within a year completed a full swim-cycle-run Ironman.

Over the nearly 40 years since then, what they achieved has proved to be within the capacity of thousands of men and women who have achieved potential they did not   know they had. They have formed the backbone of the masters and veterans classes which have developed in so many sporting activities.

When you start running or jogging you will almost certainly experience sore muscles but keep going, even at a reduced pace and distance. Allow your heart to push your blood around and raise the blood pressure, and use the exercise to flush out the waste products which are causing the muscular discomfort. You can get on the massage table but your heart will give you the best massage of all.

Hot baths help. So does turning a cold hose on your legs at the end of a run, or wading in a lake, river or the sea. Ice packs, followed by the application of heat, can help if the soreness is bothersome because the cold brings the natural cortisone to the sore areas and the heat prevents stiffness.

But if you stop running until the soreness goes you will have to got back to square one and work through sore muscles again. By maintaining the increased circulation, triggered by easy running, you will also overcome the other source of soreness which is the tearing of muscle tissues which may have become gummed together through previous lack of exercise.

9 The Technique of Running

The mechanics of running are important. Geoff Dyson's book, *The Mechanics of Athletics,* is a recommended study for the dedicated athlete but we will consider it simply here. Get the fundamentals right and we can more easily add the endurance and strength to get the maximum results.

To run correctly at speed you have got to get the knees up so that the leading thigh is as near the horizontal as possible. This enables you to stretch out further. You must also aim to bring the trailing foot up high behind you because this combined action of the legs shortens the lever established by the knee. The shorter the lever, the faster the action. The foot that comes up high behind you is going to whip through much faster than the foot that stays close to the ground. Carl Lewis had the perfect action – and the fastest speed. This very high action distinguishes the sprinter from the long-distance runner.

You can test the theory easily. Hold one end of a metre-long rod and try to move it quickly to and fro. Try it again with a 15 cm rod. The shorter rod will be easier to move fast. It is one of the reasons why we encourage what sprinters do in training – a bouncing, high knee action, as fast as possible, with the knees coming up and the other heel hitting the butt.

Caucasians, unlike the negroes, cannot get their knees up high with their hips held back and the body leaning forward, so they have to learn to run in a more upright position. However, the less you bring your upper body into the running action the better. Learn to run as you walk; arms loose, low and relaxed and moving in a straight line, the elbow flexing to let the hand come through below the hip and in a straight line.

Many women tend to run with their hands held up high at breast level, and often across the body, which wastes valuable energy and hinders forward movement by causing loss of natural balance. The arms should not play a significant role in running, which means upper body strength does not need to be developed beyond normal.

Avoid clenched fists – and a lot of people jogging for health carry small weights in clenched hands – because this tightens the shoulder muscles and causes shoulder roll. The roll throws kilos of your weight from side to side and prevents high knee striding. Relaxation, particularly of the upper body, is the key to good running.

Many people run with their legs permanently bent. They get along but they never run tall, never get the proper driving action off the front of the foot that counts. That is why our system includes exercises such as striding and bounding up a hill or stairs to encourage straight legs and develop flexible, strong ankles. The ankles produce more speed than people realise.

Running tall is important. Try to make yourself feel taller when you run. Get the feeling of always being up, not sitting in a bucket. The difference between the two is well demonstrated by today's video training methods; you can tell a runner she is sitting in a bucket but she cannot visualise it. A videotape will show the fault immediately.

When I ran training camps in the United States I used video tapes to change runners' form, within a week, from bucket-sitters to Sebastian Coes. This technique correction produced dramatic improvements.

Very few people know their true potential and they will never know until they get out and begin exercising properly. Endurance can be developed in anyone, provided they have no medical or health problems, and provided they go about it in the right way.

However, we can improve speed with better technique but we cannot make a slow person into a fast one. Efficiency and speed are always limited by the speed at which an individual can move his or her muscles. But endurance and stamina can become everyone's proud possession; perhaps not able to run a significantly fast short distance but fully capable of covering distance respectably.

As we age we begin to tighten up. Suppleness has to be regained and retained by more suppling, loosening calisthenics. Fifteen or 20 minutes a day of stretching and suppling is all I recommend.

Many injuries occur in some sports because the athlete's training concentrates on the quadriceps, the front of thigh muscles, and neglects the hamstrings behind the thighs. This imbalance can have devastating effects on the hamstrings. Note how many modern athletes take the field with thighs in elasticised bandages because they are suffering hamstring trouble. Cycling, or our scheduled programme of running upstairs and hills, balances the muscles.

Triathletes are generally trouble-free because their cycling muscles, swimming muscles and running muscles balance each other perfectly. Mark Allen, one of the world's finest triathletes, never lifted weights, never pulled a muscle. His secret was to set his bike in a high gear and head up the hills.

10 The Path to Full Potential

If you plan to step beyond the health and fitness phase and become competitive, or if you are a competitor already who wants to do better, you may find you cannot do it on your own. You need to seek the advice of a good coach or the most knowledgeable person you can find in your particular field. This help is best found by joining a club and then going to the club's best coach. Training is an individual thing because no two athletes are exactly the same; only the best coaches can evaluate those differences and devise the programmes that will strengthen the good points and eliminate the weaknesses in each individual.

You need to understand the training schedule you are following, its mechanical and psychological effects, and the reasons why the pattern has to be followed day by day to develop full potential. You must also understand that no schedule is to be slavishly followed. Schedules are guidelines which can and must be modified according to how you feel on the particular day. This does not mean skipping chunks of it and trying for a shortcut, because that will not work, but it does mean that, from time to time, the recommended intensity can be eased back without seriously affecting progress.

This book is not designed to enable you to go it alone; its purpose is to show you the right way to run, to explain why it is the right way and to set you on the road to discovering your capabilities. If that road is to be followed to its end you will need the guidance of a coach. You cannot stand back from yourself and identify where you might be going wrong or how you might effect an improvement.

A good coach will also remind you of the need for patience. Most of us cannot know how good we can be until we have been training systematically on a balanced programme for three to four years. There will be marked improvement in the first year, lesser, but no less important, improvement in the next two, and then a marked leap forward, after which you can maintain a steady rate of development.

Find your coach and place your trust in him or her, but also read everything you can about your specific sporting activity. Learn at least the basics of physiology and study the methods and techniques of others. They all contribute to the important mental fund from which you help your physical progress.

If you know why you are doing what you are doing at each phase of training, and if you understand the purpose of it, you can assess whether it is working for you. If it is not, perhaps because it is too intensive or not intensive enough, you and your coach can then steer you onto the correct alternative track.

Nothing happens overnight. Even the finest coaches can take a long time with some athletes to obtain the best results. Poor coaches can get you there fast, but they cannot continue the development along the correct lines because getting you there fast usually involves excessive anaerobic training too soon. The consequence of that is a downward curve in the development path, and usually discouragement and the loss of any hope of attaining true potential.

The smart, thinking athlete will soon know if the coach's recommended path is the wrong one because they have learnt their limitations and they can handle themselves efficiently. If they are set a specific number of repetitions or a long run, they know when the effort begins to get beyond them and they will know that is the time to quit for the day. The secret is to run those repetitions until you feel, "Well, that last one got to me. It is time to stop and cool off."

If you do not heed that inner message you risk putting in more anaerobic effort than you can handle, because the level does vary from day to day. That is what your body is telling you, so listen to it and learn to quit when it says it is time to.

My athletes never count how many reps they do, how many stride-outs, or how far and how fast they run. They give themselves proper easy days for recovery without worrying that their condition might go backwards, because they know that if they have worked out honestly there is no risk of that. They come up stronger, and in the process they have built their anaerobic capacity without setbacks.

I often set goals but my athletes and I never knew whether they reached them, stopped short or went right past them. The goals were no more than a median guide; the true requirement was that they stopped when they honestly did not feel like continuing. We lost no sleep if the schedule specified twenty 400 m reps and only nineteen were run, or if the athlete, feeling good, ran twenty-one.

This applies to all the schedules you might encounter in your running career. Slavish adherence to a schedule is inefficient. It does not necessarily achieve its physical target and it certainly does not help the mental approach because it inhibits the mind from listening to what the body is saying in the course of the exercise. If your brain is saying, "The wind and rain are making this session difficult, if not impossible", why force the body to carry on? If you are off-colour on the day, ease off or you will be even more off-colour.

The correct schedule builds to one goal after another. For instance, it is useless to go and do sprint training if you have not conditioned the muscular system to handle sprint work. Nor can you try to run five or ten kilometres fast without first building the sound aerobic conditioning base.

The cardio and blood vascular systems must be developed to what is known as the high steady state, and the muscles must be toned and strengthened before you can add power and speed without risking muscle pulls or damage.

This means you must run a big initial mileage, concentrating for as many months as possible on pure aerobic running, keeping the effort just below the point at which it overbalances into anaerobic running. The absolute minimum is three months but more time is better. This involves scheduled aerobic running plus, if you have the time – and you should determine to find that time – easy jogging, easy bouncing and springing exercises, and uphill or stairs running to apply resistance to muscle fibres.

Hill running is an important contributor to flexibility. You can use stretching exercises and some calisthenics and weight training but it should be supervised by a weights instructor and approached exactly as you do running – with caution. Gentle pressure on the system is the requirement.

11 The Competitive Athlete

After as many months of steady aerobic conditioning running as you can give yourself you move into putting more resistance in your work and at a faster pace. This involves slightly anaerobic hill training, up and down the hills, using three different exercises – bounding, springing and running – in a co-ordinated routine, and some timed hill running as well. The object is to use your weight against gravity to develop more powerful, springlike muscles, coupled with fast downhill striding to build speed. On flat sections you throw in some wind sprints to begin developing your anaerobic capacity.

This phase lasts about four weeks to ready you for the proper anaerobic training phase which will involve some harder workloads. This heavy anaerobic period also lasts about four weeks and entails three days a week of overload work in which you can do any kind of anaerobic training you like. You can run straight-out long distance hard, say from three to ten kilometres, or hard repetitions over whatever distances you feel or, if such luxuries are available, you can run hard on forest or country trails.

The repetitions can be run anywhere – on the road, in a park, on a track – and you do not need to measure the distance you are covering or count the number of times you run it. Keep up until you hit the wall. Your body tells you when you have had enough. Do not use interval training because no-one can determine exactly what anyone should do with intervals, what distance to run or the number to run. It is an obsolete training system, even though some coaches persist with it.

In conjunction with the anaerobic overload you will work on leg speed with sprint technique running and leg speed exercises.

Then, in the final six weeks, you go into co-ordination work, which gets your body used to the speed and distances at which you plan to race. You drop the long repetitions in favour of short ones, add wind sprints to sharpen the whole body and its reactions, a short, sharp technique which enables you to maintain your anaerobic capacity at the level you have achieved in earlier phases.

All this is mixed with easy fartlek – striding up and down hills, jogging, doing just what you feel like doing and enjoying the exercise, which is what fartlek (speed play) is all about. It is a valuable relief from the harder sessions.

You will also do development racing – in over-distance and under-distance events – once a week with another race adjusted according to your reactions in the previous race and the mood you are in. Every day of hard work must be followed by a day of recovery. Sessions of long stride-outs, fast but relaxed, help you to build your speed even faster.

And, once a week, you will go for a long steady run of 60 to 90 minutes. Remember that once you get into racing you do not train to train, you train to race, so the work has to be very light. Anything anaerobic is short and sharp; any long running is neither too far nor too fast.

The aim once you get into racing is to keep fresh and vital, with energy conserved for running races. You can recover from a hard race by jogging the following day, and next day doing some easy stride-outs. If you feel you need a little more sharpening, throw in some wind sprints. This way, if your conditioning background is sufficient, you can hold your form for a long time because your recovery will be excellent.

If you plan just one major race, such as a championship, or if you intend merely to enjoy a season of social running, you can mix your training, still keeping a balance, and hold your form or even continue to improve it. For this I have set out a race week/non-race week schedule which can be used for cross-country, road racing or even track racing.

This brings in all the important elements of training. In the non-race week you train harder; in the race week you back off. The hard week includes harder anaerobic volume work, some fartlek, some long aerobic running, some technique or speed training, and a couple of trials run at less than full effort to aid co-ordination. Plus, as ever, the longish easy run.

In the race week you do some short, sharp wind sprints, a little easy fartlek, an under-distance trial, and maybe some stride-outs, some jogging and a shorter long steady run.

This is a programme for people who want to enjoy their running without wanting to be champions, who want to get fun out of their running at a personally satisfying level. It does not pay to try to race ten kilometres every week, but you can easily manage that distance every third week, maybe with five kilometres races in between.

You can comfortably run a half-marathon every four or six weeks and a marathon every couple of months, provided you make sure you fully recover from each one. This is a problem area. Many people cut the recovery too short and start to bring their condition down. They get injuries and lose whatever good form they had built up, which means a return to retraining and a vast waste of time and effort. After a full or half-marathon it is wise not to do anything fast for a couple of weeks. Just jog nice and easily, with some fartlek if you feel like it. The fear that you might be losing condition is unfounded.

A lot of good marathoners last for two seasons and then fade away. They race too often, with hard 10 kms following a hard marathon for instance, maybe because they are running for money. If they make any it is likely to be a short-lived income.

The fact that, in training, you can handle a 42 km run every weekend indicates how possible it is to run a lot of marathons in a year. But when you race them all this means you come in very, very tired. You should limit yourself to no more than one every two months. The key is to recover from one before you begin setting yourself up for the next one.

The ultra-marathoner Sandra Barwick, who we have already mentioned, made a valid point when she ran her first Sydney-Melbourne road race in about seven days and, in New York only six weeks later, was the first woman to run a 1,000-miles track race. In her length-of-New-Zealand-charity-run, when she ran the Rotorua marathon in 3:54 in the course of it, she had covered 100 kilometres on each of the preceding three days; and the day after she covered 110 kilometres over a range of mountains. Before going ultra, her best marathon time was about 3:20.

12 Fitting in with the Family

Fitting scheduled training in around a family may sound daunting but regard it as a question of priorities. If running is important enough, you will make the time, whether you are a busy mother and housekeeper, a busy member of the workforce or a combination of both. Plenty of people lie around all day, or spend hours wandering through the shops, and complain they do not have time for running. All that shows is a reluctance to run.

Some people consider running boring or not worth the energy. This book is not for them, nor should you waste time trying to get them to run. Save your energy for your own roadwork.

Many thousands of those who run and achieve high mileages in training are busy people. But they find the time. Between appointments, during lunch breaks, between surgical operations, during business conferences, after work, before work. There are some out there who place such importance on running as a pleasure and a physical and mental benefit they wonder how they have time for anything else.

Joan Ullyot is a classic case of someone who found the time. She worked full-time as a doctor, cared for two children and a husband and solved the problem quite simply: "I just put running first and fit work and family in around it." It was a facetious line that, when she thought about it, contained more truth than jest.

To some it will seem a selfish credo, but nearly all serious runners are selfish, whether they are training for the Olympics or just getting up before their children to run a few kilometres every morning. The decision is justified because both work and family benefit from the vigour of the athlete.

Businessmen have discovered that a solid lunch-hour run produces better work performances than a solid lunch-hour food intake.

Families soon learn to live with a running addiction; many do by becoming addicted themselves.

There is no formula for fitting family, work and running into neat compartment. Time constraints can be tough, but if you analyse your typical day before you become a runner you will soon see where places can be made to accommodate that extra time running will need. Running to and from work is a practice widely adopted in New Zealand. Do not be deterred by the non-availability of showers, a sponge-down in a locker room or toilet where you can also change into clean clothes is usually adequate – fresh sweat is odourless – and the only real problem is to get the clean clothes there.

Non-working mothers with school-age children have no real problems. They may have to abandon one pleasure for the pleasure of running, but a quick analysis will probably show that running is almost certainly the better option in terms of well-being and wellness. These women quite often become the most avid athletes of all because the entire family is out of the way, and the activity can be carried on virtually in secret.

Joan Ullyot recorded cases of women whose families disapproved of their mother/wife running, so they stayed in dressing gown and smart hairdo until the last member of the family was gone, switched to running gear, ran as they pleased and where they pleased, returned home, even washed and dried their running clothes before the first member of the family came back through the door.

One of them, with her children at school and her husband at work, ran up to 190 km a week without their knowledge. She was allowed an hour off every weekend and that was the only time they were aware that she went for a run. Her technique was tough but effective: if she had two hours free, she ran for two hours; three hours and she ran for three.

However, her husband's antipathy to her taking time off for running was such that she had to make an excuse for leaving town when she wanted to run the Boston marathon. She left home on the Sunday, ran the Boston on the Monday in 2:58, and was home that night. Only then did she tell her husband what she had done – and he did not even ask how she fared.

Sandra Barwick got up at 4 a.m. and ran for three to four hours before getting home in time to ready her young family and husband, and herself, for school and work. They were approving of her running so at weekends she would go for runs of seven or more hours. And she was a working mother.

A mother with pre-schoolers faces a trickier problem but child care facilities are commonplace, a supportive husband can help and baby-sitters can be found for those vital times. An alternative is to take the young to a safe park, track or playing field, park them in the middle to play and run around the perimeter or the track. Even a nursing mother can find 20 to 30 minutes in a day to go running, if she plans it thoughtfully.

Be warned: running can become an obsession. It reaches the verge of that condition when you run an hour a day, or 80 km a week, because it becomes such an intrinsic part of your daily or weekly routine that you cannot go on without it. This obsession is not limited to competing athletes. It affects the woman who runs for fun but then becomes involved with testing her own capabilities, exploring her own potential. The only competition she faces is herself, but it is competition that can become quite fierce.

13 Equipment – Especially Shoes

All equipment, particularly shoes, should be examined to make sure it is suitable and will not be the cause of injury.

I emphasise the importance of shoes because healthy feet are a vital asset in most sports activities. Feet should be checked regularly for any defects – breaks in the skin, changes in shape or colour, callouses that thicken too much, athlete's foot, toe nail problems – which can worsen without quick attention and bring on serious problems.

Callouses, for instance, are natural protective layers on the feet but if they thicken they can lead to blistering underneath or cracking in dry conditions. Treatment is easy: soak any thick callouses in warm water, perhaps with a mild soap solution, for about ten minutes. Use a pumice stone or other mild abrasive to take off the extra layer but do not rub away too much. Be careful and be prepared to spend a day or three removing extra thickness. Lanolin, vaseline or a good skin lotion can be applied to prevent the foot from drying out excessively.

Breaks in the skin invite infection, and one of the worst is athlete's foot, when cracks appear between the toes and fungus develops. Careful drying and clean socks, and the use of a good ointment will get rid of this aggravating problem.

Toenails should be kept short. Long nails can damage shoes or also be pressured by shoes, leading to the unpleasant black toenail complaint. Trim toenails straight across. Leaving the corners helps to prevent ingrown toenails, which can be extremely painful and a cause of infections.

Many runners who suffer chronic problems between the toes tape their toes together, but this can create pressures, fluid build up and blisters on long runs.

Foot massage is often helpful in keeping feet in good condition.

Socks, which are merely an outer layer of skin, should always be clean and dry when they go on. Wool and cotton socks are warmer in winter and cooler in summer but wear faster than synthetics. Wool will keep sweat away from the feet, cotton absorbs it; the point being that, if you sweat a lot, wool will keep the feet dry but cotton will become soggy. Synthetic socks will also keep sweat away and tend to retain shape and cushioning effects longer: Many runners use both – a natural thin sock next to the skin and a thicker synthetic sock over it. This helps to counter the tendency of synthetic socks to overheat the feet.

Always, if you intend to wear socks when running, put them on when you are buying shoes to make sure that your feet and the shoes fit comfortably together.

Running barefoot inside your shoes offers a special closeness to the road and many runners prefer it, but it makes the feet more vulnerable to blisters and other foot abrasion problems.

Socks, it should be added, will also counter that particular pungency that running shoes get from working with bare feet.

Be careful with shoes. Badly fitting and badly laced shoes can lead to chafing, blistering and broken metatarsals (the bones between the ankles and the toes) because they do not allow the feet to function without stress. Joints, sinews and the legs generally are adversely affected by the wrong shoes and lacing.

When you try shoes on do it properly. Put the heel in and push the foot back in the shoe as far as possible. The toes must not touch the end of the shoe. When you stand you must feel that you are right on top of the shoes. The back of the shoe should not bite into the tendons, and the joint on the inside of the foot should not be touching the shoe. If you intend to have different shoes for training and running, apply the same strict rules to both.

Lace the shoes so that when they are tightened they do not pull down on the sinews and metatarsals on top of the foot. Bring the laces from front to back without crossing them diagonally across the foot. Here is how it is done: Picture the shoe facing you. Number the eyelets on the left side as 1, 3, 5, 7, 9 and so on from the toe back, and the right side eyelets as 2, 4, 6, 8 and so on. Place the ends of the lace down through eyelets 1 and 2. Do not start underneath and come upwards. Even up the ends. Take the No 1 eyelet end forward and up through eyelet 5 and then across the top of the shoe and down through eyelet 6, up underneath to eyelet 10 and straight across to eyelet 9 and up through eyelet 11. The shoelace end at eyelet 2 goes up through eyelet 4 and across to eyelet 3, underneath and up through eyelet 7, across to and down through eyelet 8, up under to eyelet 12 and there you have it. Differing numbers of shoe eyelets may force one final diagonal crossover at the front of the lace section but this does not present a problem.

In the United States this method of positioning laces has become known as the Lydiard Lace following the success a long-time Galveston, Texas, runner and writer Butch Buckner, enjoyed when he switched to it. For years, whenever he ran, his feet became numb after a few kilometres. He changed shoe styles, even tried loosening the laces but nothing succeeded. The loosened laces only gave him heel slippage and blisters. He mentioned the problem when I was in Galveston on a speaking tour. I introduced him to my lacing method and he has not only had no foot trouble since then, he has spread the message widely through his regular newspaper columns. It is now used by some of his readers for every pair of lace-up shoes they own, and has been found to be successful in reducing inflammation of the joints due to arthritic conditions.

Whatever you need for whatever sport you are pursuing, your equipment must be suitable for your age and individuality and it must be kept in good condition. One reason is that it should be a matter of pride to always be well-turned out with your gear in top order. Another is that equipment, and not just shoes, that are not looked after can lead to injuries. However, the emphasis on shoes is critical. Most sports require some form of running and the worst things that can happen can usually be traced to shoes. They do not fit, or they are off balance, because the heels have worn down, and you can run yourself into a raft of troubles, from mere blisters to the loss of toenails to major problems with your leg muscles which could seriously set back your fitness programme.

A word of caution: Women invariably have narrower feet than men so they need to buy shoes that are made in fittings for women. Men's shoe fittings could be loose on women's feet, which means the laces would have to be pulled tighter. In turn, this could lead to blood circulation being impeded or even cut off, metatarsals being damaged and sinews and muscles being injured.

So, do not buy just any shoe that seems the right price, seems to look nice – and many women's shoes have had more thought put into their feminine appearance than into their suitability for the exercise for which they are worn – and seems to fit. Different events require different kinds of shoe. Consider whether your sport involves straightforward running, side traction, twisting and turning, even running backwards or sudden starts and stops, and select your shoes accordingly.

Be careful. Shoes which have rigid soles and do not allow the foot arch to function normally should be avoided. You will never see a sprinter with flat feet, only with high arches, and the shoes must maintain that arch or speed will be lost. The good shoe sole will flex easily both ways. Try before you buy.

You need appropriate clothing for the day and the conditions, either to add warmth against cold weather or for coolness in the heat, and it must fit well. The wrong clothes can cause overheating or chills and badly fitting clothes can lead to chafing and other discomforts.

14 Diet

Millions of words have been written about diets and special foods for athletes. The advertising world goes into hyperbolical overdrive to convince athletes that this sports drink or that diet bar will accelerate their performance beyond their wildest dreams. Forget it ladies. Herbert A. de Vries, of the University of Southern California, in his book, *Physiology of Exercise*, reached this more pragmatic and practical finding: "There is no scientific evidence at the present time to indicate that athletic performance can be improved by modifying a basically sound diet ... the best diet for one athlete will seldom be the best diet for all athletes."

Once upon a time top grade footballers ate big steaks for lunch just before their matches in the belief that this would give them extra strength and stamina. The idea came down from the Greeks of the 5th century BC and it has taken a long time and a lot of research to establish its failings. Now most athletes eat lighter, balanced meals, which give them the necessary vitamins, minerals and calories. However, any sports person can suffer from dietary deficiencies even when he or she thinks the diet is properly balanced. Today's champions range from pure vegetarians to raw meat eaters.

If you are training diligently but you are not getting the results you think you should be, it makes sense to check your diet and also take a blood test for deficiencies, or a low blood count. You could be lacking in iron, calcium or some other minerals, and only proper medical tests can tell you.

Periods of hard training, for instance, call for a good intake of proteins to develop muscle tissue.

The best advice we can give is to eat the foods you feel like eating, as long as they are fresh and wholesome, rather than making big changes to foods you might not enjoy as much. If you cannot get the wholesome foods you need, take multi-vitamin tablets, even if you are not convinced of their value. In our experience vitamin supplements are definitely useful.

During aerobic exercise the body uses for energy about 48 per cent carbohydrates, 48 per cent fat acids and 4 per cent protein. In anaerobic exercise the ratio changes to about 60 per cent carbohydrates, 25 per cent fat acids and 15 per cent protein. It is apparent that the extra energy for competition comes from carbohydrates, so, for precompetition meals, the emphasis should be mainly on carbohydrates such as honey sandwiches, baked beans and so on. But give the meal time to digest, say, at least three hours before you compete.

Apart from the effect of nervous tension on the digestive system a distended stomach restricts the downward movement of the diaphragm during inhalation, and can also affect heart action by restricting the flow of blood through the heart. The first effect cuts your wind, the second reduces your endurance.

In the two days before competition, when training should be light because it is too late then to add anything to your condition, extra glucose or fructose can help to build up the body's glycogen content. During anaerobic exercise the blood sugars are burned up about 19 times faster than during aerobic training, so you must build the level as high as possible before you compete. But do not take more that 200 grams, or half a pound, of glucose or fructose during those two days.

Eating sugar within three hours of competition is unwise. The liver has to process this into glycogen and while it is doing that it will not release the glycogen it holds. However, glucose is all right but do not overdo it.

Calcium gluconate before an event, and during the training week, helps because muscle contractions require calcium ions, and if you do not provide enough you can experience cramps and nervous reactions, such as edgy, jumpy muscles which play up at night and interrupt your sleep.

During a contest or just before it, some of the specially prepared drinks supplied by pharmacies are useful because they have been developed to replace salts and minerals lost through perspiration.

The sporting fraternity has been brain-washed about the value of food supplements. They could help an athlete undergoing a heavy workload because she needs a lot of protein but they do not agree with everyone and, if they do not, they should be ignored. Upsetting your digestive system is counterproductive.

I think the best tactic is to build up your blood sugar level the day before you compete and eat sparingly on competition day, which rules out food supplements as a pregame meal.

Dr Vries reduced his sound dietary advice to these fundamentals:

1. Eat three regularly-spaced meals a day. To gain weight or prevent weight loss you can add an evening snack.
2. Eliminate as much as possible foods which furnish only calories without contributing their share of vitamins and minerals – candy, cakes, carbonated drinks, etc. – and substitute fruit and fruit juices for desserts and snacks.
3. Cut out coffee and tea which usurp more nutritious foods and can cause undesirable effects such as decreased muscular efficiency.
4. Avoid fatty foods which slow gastric emptying.
5. Eat two servings of fresh fruit a day. One serving should be citrus fruits or tomatoes.

6. Eat vegetables every day, including leafy, green vegetables (salads) and roots and tubers (turnips, beet, potatoes, etc.).
7. Eat at least three slices of wholegrain bread a day.
8. Eat enough butter or fortified margarine to supplement the bread.
9. Drink at least three glasses of milk a day.

Watch your salt consumption. Small doses are eliminated quickly but large doses stay in the body tissues and blood stream, causing hyperchloremia. Research has shown that the Indians of America, the Eskimoes and the people of interior China, none of whom ate salt, were perfectly healthy. Salt is not necessary for life. In small doses it is a stimulant, like coffee, tobacco, alcohol and morphine, and can become concentrated in the blood and body tissues so that its sudden discontinuation can violently upset the nervous balance.

Stirring the adrenalin with stimulants can make you feel better, but it is an effect of exhilaration that only emphasises underlying fatigue.

In hot weather you need plenty of liquid. Electrolytes are valuable.

Calcium or dolomite are important to eliminate the cause of muscle cramps when you are training and competing hard.

A balanced diet is essential for full sporting development. You cannot capitalise fully on your training and exercise regimes if you are not giving your body the correct foods. Some people who ignore a balanced diet and eat a lot of fast foods may get away with it for some years, but it can lead to health problems later. Good wholesome foods, such as fresh fruit, vegetables and lean meats in moderation, have to become the norm. You may envy the fast food munchers at the start but they will envy you when you prove your vastly superior physical build and ability.

A word of caution. Many supermarket vegetables are grown in artificial fertiliser solutions and lack trace elements, such as chromium, zinc and selenium, so young athletes should be taking multi-vitamin and mineral tablets to overcome the deficiencies.

Next, let us consider the vitamins and minerals topic in a little more detail.

15 Vitamins and Minerals

If we all ate the same food life could become fairly boring. Children already tend to apply that description to any food placed before them with the instruction, "Eat it up. It is healthy." The influences of the manufacturers and sellers of fast, convenience or junk food – call it what you will – have helped to create that attitude.

Their products, it has to be admitted, score highly on taste, flavour and availability, but they fall well short of what growing youngsters should be eating.

Many foodstuffs we think of as good for us have been processed to the point where it is uncertain what they are; and the origins of much of our fruit and vegetables are unknown. Fresh fruit and vegetables are valuable in our diet but, if the soil in which they were grown lacks the trace elements we need for a balanced diet, we can be assured that the produce is also lacking. We need selenium, zinc, chrome and cobalt, which should be natural elements of our soil. The amounts we need are small but they are vital. Unfortunately modern agricultural methods, with their heavy dependence on artificial fertilisers and intensive cropping, have removed most of those elements.

I have never been a fan of supplements but, if you cannot be sure the food you eat contains everything your body needs, you have to turn to multi-vitamin and mineral supplements. This does not mean we become pill-poppers pouring mega doses of tablets into our systems, but we need to check our diet carefully, know the sources of our foods and understand how we can overcome deficiencies if we want to give our metabolism the chance to perform all its functions efficiently. This is particularly important when your physical and mental energy outputs are consistently high. We cannot rely on our croppers and farmers to do that for us, although more and more are becoming conscious of the need to upgrade and maintain the nutritional values of their land and their stock in a world which is increasingly health-minded.

Watch out for additives in processed food. It has long been recognised that manufacturers who added food colourings, additives and preservatives could be pouring a highly toxic mix into the stomachs of their consumers, which could lead to all sorts of cancerous, arthritic and other problems. Dr Curatin, one of the recognised health experts in the United States, discussing this with me in the 70s, asked what parents were thinking when they gave their children iceblocks which coloured their tongues purple or green or red. Did they pause to consider what those toxic colouring agents were doing to them?

It has been found since that some of the red dyes used to make food seem more attractive are actually carcinogenic. And many more sophisticated additives have been developed since Dr Curatin raised the issue nearly three decades ago.

For instance, Gary and Steven Null disclosed in a book in 1977 that 90 per cent of food manufacturers' colourings were synthetic and most were derived from coal-tar. Even Florida oranges were dyed. So were dog foods, although dogs are colour-blind. The lure is for the dogs' owners.

Consider the American chicken. To kill all bacteria, even beneficial bacteria, the food with which chickens are force-fed is laced with drugs, including arsenic, and antibiotics. To keep them calm, they are given tranquilisers. They are fattened in about half the time it used to take, so the meat they produce is pasty white and bland, and artificial dyes have been developed to colour the flesh golden, and the enzyme hyaluronidase is injected to add flavour. Because the enzyme would smell acrid during cooking it is masked with a seasoning mixture of herbs and garlic.

Compare this with the diet followed by the great African runners – natural unprocessed foods taken from ground which has not been overcropped or over-grazed and remains rich in trace elements.
Some years ago, in San Diego Zoo, several bears died of cancer. The cause was the processed food they were being given.

Modern nutrition is a controversial subject because it can never be an exact science. People are constantly caught between the dietitians who extol the world's natural balanced diets and the health foodshop owners who would have you believe you need the help of every pill, powder and potion on their shelves. Both sides are, in some respects, correct.

The American magazine *Women's Sports*, after studying nutrition for four years, concluded that just about everyone needs to take vitamin supplements. You need them if you live in a smoggy city, if you train regularly in heat, if you eat sugar, if you have an allergy, if you load on carbohydrates before a competition, if you bruise easily.

"Life is action", the magazine said, "There is nothing static about the body. What sparks and controls that action – the beating of your heart, the steady fire of digestion, your breathing, your moving – are enzymes. Vitamins are a chemical part of your enzymes. Without vitamins your enzymes wouldn't work, and neither would you.

For instance, without thiamin (vitamin B_1), the brain and nervous system collapse. Arms and legs lose their co-ordination. The eye muscles freeze into paralysis. The mind blackens into amnesia and coma. The heart stretches, swells – and stops."

Scary stuff perhaps, but true. So let's run through the vitamins from the viewpoint of athletic performance:

Vitamin A is the one vitamin on which you can overdose, but you would have to take huge daily amounts, because unused vitamin A is stored in the liver. It is also the vitamin people get the least of if they do not eat enough fresh fruit and vegetables but do eat too much fast or convenience food. Vitamin A keeps the skin smooth, the vision sharp, the immune system strong, and anti-stress mechanisms on the ball. Dry, rough or flaky skin is an indicator of A deficiency.

Find it in orange, yellow and green fruits and vegetables (carrots, sweet potatoes, spinach, apricots and cantaloupe). These contain betacarotene, which may be killed by overcooking but changes to vitamin A once it gets into the body. Fish liver oil is the most concentrated source. Vitamin A supplements, because they are tasteless and odourless, are the best source of fish liver oil. If you also take vitamin E, the body's ability to use A increases sixfold.

B-complex takes care of anything that gets on your nerves. Depression, irritability, poor concentration, insomnia, forgetfulness, confusion, anxiety and paranoia are all linked to some extent with B-complex vitamins, which go together as a family. B_1 (thiamin) helps to turn carbohydrates into glucose to fuel the brain and the muscles. Five milligrams of thiamin a day will turn all pasta into energy for instance, which makes it important for "carbo" loaders.

Green leafy vegetables, wholegrains, beans, nuts and seeds are thiamin-rich and also contain all the other Bs except B_{12}.

B_2 (riboflavin) helps the digestion of fats and is found in broccoli, asparagus, milk, cheese, almonds, liver and any wholegrain. Wild rice is best.

Some 40 chemical reactions in the body depend on **B_3 (niacin)**. The most important involve the red blood cells which take oxygen to all parts of the body. The last stage of their journey is through the capillaries, hair-thin blood vessels connecting to the tissues. The blood cells line up in single file and march in, each separated from its neighbour by a negative electrical charge. Niacin keeps them charged and they keep the body charged.

B_{12} (cobalamin) helps to run the switchboard of the central nervous system, relaying messages between the body and the brain. The best source is liver but any animal product will do. Interestingly, vegans (total vegetarians) who eat fermented foods such as tamari or tofu or large amounts of raw food, manufacture B_{12} in their own intestinal tracts.

Folate, best found in green leafy vegetables, particularly from the cabbage family, but also in wholewheat, brewer's yeast, oranges, beets, beans, meat and eggs, helps to form genes, the chemicals that blueprint every cell. Folate deficiency is a cause of anaemia.

Pantothenic acid is needed if you train, compete or even play in cold weather. It exists in all foods except canned and frozen foods and anything made with white flour, which may lose up to 75 per cent of pantothenic acid.

Choline and **inosotol** are two B vitamins in **lecithin,** a substance that is part of the cell walls of plants and animals. They make sure the cells absorb fat, which is as vital a nutrient as protein or carbohydrate.

Vitamin C is so strong it detoxifies heroin, nicotine, alcohol and cancer-causing pollutants. One gram every two hours will cure the common cold. It also beats the heat; increasing your C intake a week or so before an event in hot weather will improve your competitive edge. Fresh oranges, all citrus fruits, potatoes, green peppers, parsley and broccoli are rich in C but not frozen or bottled juices. Potato chips have lost about 75 per cent of vitamin C.

Bioflavinoids are closely related to C and their main value is that they strengthen capillaries. The white inner skin of citrus fruits and the white column inside a green pepper are packed with them.

Vitamin E's sole purpose is to absorb calcium but, since calcium regulates muscle contractions, the heart could not beat without it. Little is acquired from eating. It comes from sunlight, so, unless you hide completely from the sun, you should not be in danger of deficiency. E helps glycogen storage, giving you more fuel for endurance; protects cells from oxidation, cleans up chapped lips, surgical incisions, burns (including sunburn), bedsores, warts, athlete's foot, poison ivy and any skin complaint.

Processed foods are almost lacking in E. Cornflakes, for instance, have lost all but two per cent. Wholewheat bread has seven times more than white bread, brown rice six times more than white.

We carry about 1.3 kg of **calcium**, mostly in bones and teeth, but if we removed the remaining one-tenth of one per cent from our circulatory systems, our muscles would not contract. The mechanism regulating the level of that small but vital amount of calcium is so exact that, if the amount drops a microgram or two too low, calcium is immediately taken from the bones to cover the deficit. A calcium lack affects nerves and muscles as well as bones and teeth, hence muscle cramps.

Women in particular need calcium because it is vital in checking osteoporosis, which hobbles millions of the elderly, a high percentage of whom are women. Calcium should probably become a regular supplement from about age 25 when bone loss begins. It has been calculated that calcium supplementation begun then would give a 70-year-old the bone mass and strength of a 40-year-old. For the athlete, calcium reduces the risk of a stress fracture.

Best calcium sources are bone meal, cottage cheese, Swiss cheese, yoghurt, sardines and salmon, collard and turnip green, tofu and, according to macrobiotic enthusiasts, a green tea called Bancha which, they claim, has more calcium than milk. Milk, however, is a questionable source because of its accompanying fats and calories, and because many people cannot easily digest it.

Dolomite (see below) is a great calcium supplement.

Phosphorus exists in all the cells in your body and in every biochemical reaction. Equally with calcium it keeps your skeleton sturdy, assists your heart beat, your digestion and purification through the kidneys and the nervous system. Nearly everybody now gets too much and since it needs to be virtually a one-to-one ratio with calcium, you need to use calcium supplements and watch your meat intake – meat has a phosphorus to calcium ratio of about 209 to 9.

If you toss and turn at night turn to **magnesium**. This natural tranquiliser calms jumpy muscles and nerves. It is also needed for the digestion of protein, fats and carbohydrates. Good sources are wholegrains, soybeans, nuts, leafy green vegetables, fruit and blackstrap molasses, but the best of all is **dolomite**, a preparation of powdered dolomite limestone which delivers magnesium and calcium in the exact proportions nature intended.

Athletes who do not sweat do not need extra **potassium**; those who do and take salt tablets need double doses. Research has established that half of people hospitalised for heat stroke after intense exercise are potassium-depleted. Many have taken salt tablets which forced the potassium from their bodies, and this, added to potassium lost through sweating, produced a severe deficiency with all its symptoms – nausea, muscle weakness, cramps, irritability and, finally, collapse.

You need about 2,000 mg of **sodium** a day – a typical salt-shaker diet delivers from 10,000 to 12,000 mg. Solve that by filling your salt shaker with natural spices and eat natural unprocessed foods. They deliver a natural amount of sodium and taste better. Excess salt is thought to contribute to high blood pressure, which is bad news for athletes training in hot weather.

Iron is used to fortify cereals, baked goods and other processed foods, but the body absorbs less than one per cent of it. The only source of iron the body will accept is vitamin C, and 1,000 mg with a meal will boost absorption tenfold. The iron in meat also helps the absorption of iron from other foods, but processed foods often contain additives and preservatives which block iron absorption. Tea's tannic acid shifts iron out of the body, and so does regular use of aspirin.

Research has shown that people with normal blood levels of iron, who added iron to their diet, boosted their work capacity four times, which should be significant for hard-working athletes. But be sparing, it is possible to overdose. The vitamin C should be enough, plus no more than about 20 mg of an iron supplement.

Chromium helps the body to use insulin, the hormone that regulates blood sugar (glucose). If you eat 120 pounds (54 kg) of sugar a year – as many do even in these enlightened days – you need lots of insulin to burn the sugar and lots of chromium to help the process. The finest source is brewer's yeast and about two tablespoons a day is recommended.

Almost nothing happens in the body without **zinc**, which is vital for normal sexual maturation, speeds the healing of burns and all kinds of wounds, helps to stop the absorption of lead and protects against cadmium. Oysters contain 100 times more zinc than any other food but good sources are red meat, liver, wheat germ and nuts. Unless you "pig out" on oysters, a 20 mg a day zinc supplement is recommended.

Found in seafood, wholegrains, organ meats and brewer's yeast, **selenium** is hailed as a nutritional cancer preventive and stroke stopper. As evidence of this, people in an area of Georgia and the Carolinas, which has less selenium per capita than anywhere else in the United States, have more strokes per capita than anywhere else. It is a must for normal bones and muscles and is best found in beans, peas, spinach, bran, brussels sprouts and blueberries.

16 Changes to the Body

For many years, controversy has raged over whether running can damage women. Sterility has been one issue, largely discounted; physical damage another, dispelled by the achievements of the modern female runner.

Menstrual irregularity has been a subject of debate for a long time and has been suspected to be especially frequent among long-distance runners. When Joan Ullyot discussed this with elite women runners in America and Europe, each thought her own lack of periods was unique and each was reluctant to consult a non-running, male gynaecologist about it. Most of these women were in their early twenties.

An earlier survey of forty-seven young distance runners, most of them teenagers, revealed eleven had very irregular periods, but irregularity is notorious among the young, which made the finding inconclusive.

Subsequent studies showed top-level American women runners averaged significantly fewer periods (8.1 a year) than non-running but athletic and sedentary groups (11.4 a year). Irregularity was less common among runners but was reported by 51 per cent of non-mothers.

So, if you are having scanty, delayed or absent periods since you took up distance running, you are not unique and, says Joan Ullyot, enlightened gynaecologists, trained to recognise good health, would conclude that the absence of periods was simply a reflection of good physical condition and not a cause for worry.

As for the threat of infertility through running, the evidence is reassuring to would-be mothers. The absence of periods is not permanent and is no indication of sterility. In fact, a woman who is having irregular, or no periods, should never assume she is infertile and depend on this for birth control. Joan Ullyot records several cases where women runners became pregnant without having a period. The absence of menstruation does not indicate that ovulation is not occurring, only that it is irregular and unpredictable at times.

Millions of women around the world now run or jog on a regular basis. Since most are in their child-bearing years it is no surprise that many of them become pregnant each year. Nor is it unexpected, given the addictive nature of running, that they want to keep running as long as possible.

The good news is that, as long as they walk or jog at a comfortable aerobic pace, which means they can talk as they run if they want to, they are doing themselves more good than harm. It is possible to run right up to term, as comfort dictates. Pregnancy will slow you down but it is not a barrier to a vigorous life-style.

Joan Ullyot cites the case of a "strong, slim, radiant" young woman who, three weeks before her baby was born, ran a half-marathon in 2:10, at 10-minute-mile pace. The baby's remarkable disposition was credited to the fact that, as a foetus, it lived in a calm, healthy and well-oxygenated environment.

For the pregnant woman, regular aerobic activity helps to lower water retention and weight gain, improves muscle tone, and accelerates postpartum recovery. The psychological benefit is probably equally important.

As for the unborn child being bounced around and possibly harmed, it should be remembered that it lives not in a backpack but in its own personalised, watery, warm internal environment, cushioned against shock.

It is also a recorded fact that the newborn babies of running mothers score universally high marks for alertness, colour and good disposition. One reason is that running increases oxygen uptake, which is the consumption of air by muscles as opposed to intake, which is the consumption of air by the lungs. When you run your heart rate increases, cardiac output more than doubles, and oxygen consumption can rise eight times above the resting level. It is now widely accepted that the foetus enjoys its full share of the extra daily oxygen.

Running during pregnancy does require some precautions – a more supportive bra, some form of abdominal support, such as a wide bandage, liberal use of petroleum jelly over all friction points and between the thighs and more attention to the cushioning and support of your running shoes.

Interestingly, many serious women runners have actually improved their performances after having a baby. The first American woman to run the 800 metres under two minutes, Madeline Manning Jackson, did so after bearing a child. The East Germans found that women who had given birth could tolerate higher workloads than their peers who had not. They actually encouraged women athletes to have a child sometime in the two years before the Olympics.

How will you look as a serious runner? You may be young at heart and young of body but will you look younger than you are? The improved circulation and oxygen flow will help to maintain good skin tone and quality, but the environment you run in is not always kind. Sun, heat, cold all have an effect, and continued distance running produces hollow cheeks, leanness, and takes away the subcutaneous fat which fills the skin of young girls and lends them that unwrinkled bloom of youth. The fat loss means skin lines will show more readily.

It pays to cover up when you run in the sun. A visor to shield the face and ample sunscreen, preferably not of the oil type, are important.

17 Injury Avoidance and Treatment

It is almost inevitable that, no matter how careful you are or how physically fit you may be, you will experience some injuries from time to time. Some will arise from pure accident, some could be caused by inattention to your own well-being.

For instance, watch heel wear on your running shoes closely. Excessive wear will lead to stress right up through the leg and hip and can also cause bone wear; you may not always be aware what is happening until it becomes a real problem. Lost heel rubber should be replaced as often as once a month.

What I have said about the modern running shoe was supported in 1990 by two researchers from the Human Performance Group in the Mechanical Engineering Department at Concordia University in Montreal. Their studies through the 1980s made the startling discovery that barefoot running in subjects who normally wore shoes resulted in greater shock-moderating behaviour than when they were wearing any of the running shoes that were tested.

Modern running shoes, they concluded, were no better than and were sometimes worse than the unadapted barefoot in reducing shock during running. In fact, other research showed that the more expensive athletic shoes from major manufacturers were particularly dangerous to use, and produced a higher incidence of injuries.

The reason was that the excessive cushioning and gimmickry used in the shoes created illusions of protection which tricked the body into not making the shock-absorbing reactions which the normal human organism makes automatically when running in bare feet. They could lead the athlete to run with greater impact, increasing the shock effect and the risk of damage.

Athletes tend to get a lot of knee problems because most of them spend a lot of time on cambered roads. Try to avoid that side-angled running if you can. Similarly, shoes which are not laced tightly can roll under the feet. Both result in possible damage to the meniscus and cartilage in the knee. This is not an immediate injury and may take years to develop, but always bear in mind that it can happen and take precautions.

Some leg problems can be quite complex in their cause and cure so do not play around with an injury if you do not know exactly what it is and it does not recover quickly. Get yourself to an expert.

A common knee injury is **chondramalacia**, which is felt just below the patella (kneecap). The invariable cause is the failure to stretch the quadriceps before exercising. The quads are powerful muscles, and if they are still tight when you begin running, they will not stretch as you bend your knees, which will pull the tendons. These are anchored on soft bone under the knee and the strain is the result.

The stretching is easy. Either do squats or stand alongside a fence or wall, supporting yourself against it, and swing the inside leg backwards and forwards, alternating between a bent and a straight knee. Keep this exercise going for both legs until you feel comfortable and relaxed in the muscles and sinews of the upper leg. The prevention is so much easier than the cure.

Those strong quads, the front of the thigh muscles, are often the cause of **hamstring pulls,** because the hams have not been developed to the same extent and cannot take the strain when the quads are used to lift the legs through fast. Again, the cure is simple enough: get hams and quads into balance by hill or stair running, not fast but with a good knee lift so that you feel the resistance on the muscle you are trying to strengthen. This is not the bouncing action we do more for ankle strength and flexibility but slow positive upwards running.

Jogging, or easy running, is unlikely to damage a hamstring. It hits when you begin sprinting.

Muscle tears are damage to the muscle sheath. You can usually place your finger right on the damaged and tender point of the tear. It means the muscle will not contract and, depending on how bad the tear is, can be quite painful. The treatment is to make the area as cold as possible as soon as possible to stop internal bleeding, because the more blood seeps out between the muscle sheaths the longer you are going to have getting over it. Do not use massage for at least four days, and preferably do not use it then, either.

Run onto a stone or into a hole, slip on the stairs or a roadside kerb and the resultant scream of pain tells you you have suffered a **sprain**. If it is a bad one it will swell up quickly, so again it needs ice as soon as you can apply it, followed by compression (tight bandaging). And then, if you can, use it. Do not put it up and rest it. I have proved many times that most sprains recover faster if you keep going. A sprain is almost always a minor injury and, if you can run through the initial pain, it may vanish completely within a hundred metres or so. It will get worse if you stop and feel sorry for yourself. However, if running does not cure it, you need the ice and compression treatment and then get back into action carefully.

Blisters can become a problem if they open up – you might have to do this yourself if they are large. Always bathe them with disinfectants and keep medication on to prevent them becoming septic. Blisters can often be traced to the wrong kind of socks, if you wear them, or to foot movements within your shoes because you have not laced them properly, or they are the wrong shape or size. Blistering under the foot – we call it hot foot – is normally caused because shoes have not been put on properly. It is important that when you put them on to jam your heels as far back as they will go and then lace the shoes up firmly. Start running with even an eighth of an inch (3 cm) gap between your heel and the back of the shoe and you set the scene for friction, which causes heat, which can cause the skin to break. This can be particularly damaging when you are running downhill. The foot will crush forward and you could lose a toenail.

Swelling feet, which happens to some extent during running, need never be a problem. Stop and quickly loosen the laces, and then get running again. Remember that although the foot might swell slightly sideways it will not swell longways.

Chafing in the crotch, across the chest or under the arms needs the same careful attention to avoid infection, and it is best to anticipate the problem and use olive oil, petroleum jelly or some similar lubricant to prevent it.

Many years ago Dr Jack Sinclair, who was a New Zealand mile champion, researched the **stitch problem** and made the odd discovery that people riding camels got stitch because their diaphragms were bouncing up and down with the camel's motion and extending the ligaments that hold the diaphragm to the skeleton underneath the rib case. This helps to explain why stitch strikes the runner going downhill and experiencing increased jarring.

You can do sit-ups to strengthen the muscles in that area but, if you do not do backbending as well, you will produce tight, inelastic muscles which will cramp the heart and lungs when they expand.

Good suppling and stretching techniques are: chesting a table edge, or similar exercises, for the entire area where flexibility and elasticity are vital; and hip rotation exercises.

Many runners get **back problems** and try to correct them by forward stretching exercises. That is fine for the outer back muscles but the inner muscles closer to the spine also need work and must be stretched the other way. Uphill running does that or you can use light weights. Again, the main requirement is back-bending, but you need to hold the position for at least a minute to get real benefit.

Cramp is a common problem and the cause is usually a lack of calcium. Very little calcium is used for muscle contraction and the central nervous system, but if you do not have enough for both it will be taken from your bones which will weaken your skeletal structure. The best way to take calcium is with vitamin D as a catalyst and preferably in a gluconate form for easy absorption into the system.

A calcium deficiency is also a cause of **stress fractures** because, if you take calcium out of your bones they cannot take the steady pounding of distance running or hard exercise.

You will know when you get a **metatarsal stress fracture** because, quite simply, you will not be able to run properly, if at all, and the pain will be severe. An immediate X-ray will not reveal the problem; you need to wait ten days or so. It is important, if you think you have damaged a metatarsal, to go to your doctor or physio at once. You cannot fix this one yourself.

Shin splints have several causes. A common one is shoes that are too rigid so that when the runner's heel hits the ground the whole foot claps down instead of rolling through flexibly from heel to toe. This is particularly noticeable in steep downhill running when tight front shin muscles are stretched too quickly, and the membrane between the muscle and the bone ruptures. Tight ankle muscles, which do not allow the ankle to flex properly, and tight muscles under the calves, also pull the muscle sheaths.

Blood circulation in the shin area is not good so recovery from shin splints can be slow. Again use ice and, if you want to continue running, stay on the flat, preferably on grass. Whatever you do do not run downhill. Again, a physio can help you but, because recovery can take so long in some cases, prevention is a million times better than the cure. Work on ankle flexibility as mentioned earlier. Standing on a step or stair on the balls of the feet and lifting up and down fully extends sinews and muscles at the back and front of the legs. Later, when you are ready for it, uphill bounding or springing will work exceptionally well for both ankle and foot flexibility. Like any other exercise it is one that has to be worked on steadily.

Bursitis at the back of the heel occurs with running shoes which bite in just underneath the Achilles' tendon. If you damage flesh and bone a gristly growth forms on the bone and can grow and reach the stage where it pushes on the Achilles' tendon itself. People with bulbous heels are less at risk than the straight up and down heel type. Fortunately more and more running shoes are made these days with a u-shaped cutaway at the heel to eliminate this problem. But, if you feel shoe pressure at your heels, be warned.

A bursar that gets too big will require surgical removal, which is inevitably successful, but if the bursar is small and you avoid aggravating it, you can probably live with it.

Bunions do not need to interrupt training and you can cut a hole in your shoe to let a bunion, which is a growth on the bone itself, have its freedom. Just make sure the edges of the hole are softened. It is not a pretty sight and it is a rough way to treat expensive shoes, but it will work until you get rid of the bunion.

Heel spurs, which are also growths on the bone, are an awkward problem. I developed one by jamming my heel down on some hard object. My doctor wanted to operate but I was not having any of that. I went home, cut a hole in the inner bottom of the shoe so the spur would fit into it and had been running for a month before I realised I could not feel it any longer. It had gone.

But heel spur can be a painful condition and, if my rough-and-ready method, again tough on the shoe, does not work, seek medical advice.

Cartilage and meniscus troubles in the knee occur in several sports, particularly in games such as football which call for quick twisting and turning at speed. What happens is that while the body is turning and rotating the foot is firmly anchored to the ground by the sprigs of its boot. The meniscus, the pad inside the knee, and the cartilage, which goes around the bone, take the full wrenching strain. Running can produce these injuries, and jarring and pounding in shoes that are not resilient enough can wear down the meniscus and weaken the grip between bone and cartilage.

A damaged meniscus or cartilage may have to be removed but it does not mean an end to running. Barry Magee, who was bronze medalist in the 1960 Olympic marathon, is now in his sixties and still running well, although his cartilages have gone long ago. But he takes good care of himself, as every runner should.

Elasticised bands are something of a statement on thighs, knees and ankles these days, but they can grip on the skin and cause rawness. They must flex freely at the joints and they should not roll up. The Americans use a type of surgical stocking supplied in long rolls rather like cheesecloth. They cut enough off to cover any area they want protected, and can even double or treble the thickness. The beauty of it is that it does not bunch up and become a nuisance when you are moving.

18 Setting out Your Schedule

Choose your most important race date and count back the days before it. Allow six weeks for co-ordination, four weeks for anaerobic development, four weeks for hill resistance training. The time left before these phases is for conditioning training.

Conditioning starts with only aerobic mileage over flats and hills. Then you include a day of easy fartlek and strong runs over, say, 3 or 6 kms every alternate week.

Hill training is two or three days weekly, with one day for a long aerobic run and the other days for leg speed and fast relaxed runs over 100 metres. Some wind sprints should be thrown in every 15 minutes during hill training.

Anaerobic training takes place two or three days a week, with one day for a long aerobic run, and the others for sprint training and easy running. It is a hard-easy-hard-easy method.

The schedules also include sharpeners, trials, development races (over- and under-distance), pace judgement training, fast relaxed striding and, if needed, some fast anaerobic 300 and 500 metres runs.

Freshening up is an important factor.

These are what the various terms used in the schedules mean:

Long aerobic running means you train at a fairly strong aerobic effort, not just jogging. It does NOT mean racing your training. In theory you should be running at 70% to 100% of your aerobic capacity. Finish in a pleasantly tired state.

Easy fartlek running means easy 'speedplay'. Run over undulating areas if possible, mixing in some fast stride-outs, hill sprints, downhill striding, sustained runs for a minute or two, or whatever you feel like doing without tiring yourself too much. Jog easily between the faster parts whenever you feel like it. It should be enjoyable exercise. Parks and golf courses are ideal, but do not interfere with other users of the areas.

Strong fartlek running is similar to easy, just a little more strenuous, and is used to develop your anaerobic capacity to exercise. You should finish in a tired state.

Hill springing is used to strengthen the legs and the ankles in particular. Find a gentle slope and, after warming-up, go up the hill using a bouncing action with slow forward momentum. Push hard off the toes to lift your centre of gravity. Come down on the toes of the other foot, allowing your ankle to flex, thereby stretching the tendons and muscles.

Your body weight acts as a form of resistance and helps to develop the fast twitch or white muscle fibres, helping in speed development. It is important to have strong and flexible ankles to gain the optimum speed possible. You should only do what your legs can take, initially a little and then gradually increasing the workload.

A little done frequently can help.

Bounding uphill with high knees and a straight back leg helps to develop power and drive.

Hill springing: vital for leg strengthening, with special benefit for the ankles. Push hard off the toes, land on the toes to flex the ankles fully. The forward movement is minimal.

Steep hill or steps running is used mainly to strengthen the thigh muscles, although the whole leg benefits. Knee lift is important in running at all distances, from sprints to the marathon. The quadriceps (front thigh muscles) often tire and cause the runner to lose stride length and leg speed. Do only what you can manage, giving your legs a good recovery before doing more of the exercise. Run up a steepish hill or steps, bringing your knees up to make the back leg drive fairly hard. Do not try to go up too fast. Make your legs feel the workload. One variation: using a more gentle slope, run up quite fast with long, high, knee-lifting strides, forcing your arms through fast. Always take a good recovery jog before striding downhill again. The length of the hill or steps should be more than 100 metres if possible.

Hill bounding: more effective than level bounding, with emphasis on straight back leg and strong arm drive. Studies 5 and 6, from behind, highlight the vigour of the arm movements.

Bounding: with high knees and a straight back leg, this is an exercise to develop power and drive and the all-important knee lift. It is in effect a series of long leaps.

Leg speed is fast running over about 100 metres. Concentrate on using your quadriceps and lower stomach muscles to pull your legs through **quickly.** Try to maintain a near-normal stride length.

Then jog easily for 300 metres before repeating. **Always run the fast work with the wind at your back.**

Sprint training consists of warming-up, stretching and doing three specific exercises (over about 100 metres) to concentrate on form (see below). Then combine the ingredients in all three exercises and run over the 100 metres twice, as fast and relaxed as you can, with a jogging interval after each. After this, run round the track up to six times, using one straight to run fast and relaxed with a 300-metres jogging interval. The three ingredients are:

High knee lift, in which you aim for slow forward momentum, raising the knees high and fast in a running action so that the quadriceps begin to feel tired. Do what you feel you can. Jog back easily and repeat.

Long striding, lift your knees high, taking long strides, forcing your arms through and driving hard off the back foot. Do this twice with good recovery intervals.

And **running tall**, in which you keep high on the toes, lifting your knees high and stretching your body upwards to lift your torso from your pelvis. Do this twice and take the necessary recovery. The running speed should not be too fast; concentrate on keeping up tall.

Stretching and suppling: These exercises are important before and after athletic effort. First, to stretch muscles and tendons easily and stimulate blood flow; afterwards, to ease muscles which have been under stress and to help the body to get rid of any wastes generated by running.

Pulling up on the raised back foot, full back and forward leg swings, across-the-body toe touching and rhythmic circular hip rotation, all shown here, will work on all parts of the body and limbs.

High knees: sprinters use this exercise. All runners should. Forward momentum is slow as the knees are raised high and fast in an exaggerated almost on-the-spot running action. ➞

Striding: the objective of striding, which is used in sprint training, is to lift the knees high and take long strides while forcing the arms through and driving hard off the back foot.

45-metres wind sprints every 200 metres are used for sharpening and to develop the ability to deal with changes in the pace of racing. From the start put markers at 0 metres, 25 metres, 70 metres and 95 metres. Sprint hard for the 45 metres (from 25 to 70 or vice versa), then jog around the 0-95 markers and back to the start of the 45-metre sprint.

100-metres wind sprints every 200 metres are similar to the preceding exercise in effect but are more effective anaerobically. Sprint the straights and float the bends of the track.

Reps are for anaerobic capacity development. Run one and jog one.

Time trials are to co-ordinate training. They are run at about seven-eighths effort throughout. Do not sprint at the end.

Pace judgement running is used over 400 metres in 4 to 6 repetitions. Try to run at the speed you intend to average in your racing. Take whatever interval you feel you need for recovery as it is important to run the exact time if possible – not over or under.

Relaxed striding teaches you how to race relaxed. Continually running varying distances from 100 to 300 metres, keeping the upper body relaxed and concentrating on running with good technique, will help you to run faster times without being basically fitter. The pace is easy.

Fast relaxed striding is similar to relaxed striding but is run at your best relaxed speed.

Calisthenics involves any exercise that you feel will help, such as sit-ups and push-ups.

Skipping rope with a running action can be valuable when the weather does not allow you to train outdoors. It has good value for oxygen uptake development.

Cycling is good for running and can be used if you are injured. It is also helpful for leg speed.

Swimming can be used during and for injury recovery, though not too much is recommended for runners.

Jogging is very easy running.

Sprint starts are exactly that and are useful practice for the shorter race distances.

19 The Schedules

Conditioning

This schedule is for cross-country and road race preparation. The variations in time and/or distance are the minimums and maximums, governed by how the runner feels on the day.

For ten weeks or more

Monday:	Aerobic 45/60 minutes.
Tuesday:	Aerobic 60/75 minutes.
Wednesday:	Run hilly course 30/60 minutes.
Thursday:	Aerobic 60/90 minutes.
Friday:	Jog 30/60 minutes.
Saturday:	Run hilly course 30/60 minutes.
Sunday:	Aerobic 60/120 minutes.

For four weeks

Monday:	Run hilly course 30/60 minutes.
Tuesday:	Aerobic 60/90 minutes.
Wednesday:	Trial 2,000/3,000 metres.
Thursday:	Aerobic 60/90 minutes.
Friday:	Relaxed striding 200 metres 4/8 times.
Saturday:	Trial 3,000/5,000 metres.
Sunday:	Aerobic 60/120 minutes.

Hill Training

For four weeks

Monday: Leg speed 100 metres by 6/10 times.
Tuesday: Hill exercises 15/60 minutes.
Wednesday: Fast relaxed running 100 metres 6/10 times.
Thursday: Hill exercises (or jog) 15/60 minutes.
Friday: Leg speed 100 metres 6/10 times.
Saturday: Aerobic 60/120 minutes.
Sunday: Aerobic 60/120 minutes.

Anaerobic Training

For four weeks

Monday: Sprint training.
Tuesday: Reps.
Wednesday: Easy fartlek 30/60 minutes (jogging, striding and sprinting according to mood).
Thursday: Reps or jog.
Friday: Relaxed striding, fast and easy.
Saturday: Reps.
Sunday: Aerobic 60/120 minutes.

Co-ordination Training

For eight weeks

Monday: Sharpeners.
Tuesday: For middle distance – fast relaxed striding out or sprint training according to mood.
               For distance – 2,000/3,000 metres time trial.
               For either – easy fartlek or aerobic run up to 60 minutes.

Wednesday:	Development races or trials; a sprint and middle distance.
Thursday:	Fast relaxed striding – pace judgement – easy fartlek – fast runs in reps over 300 metres by 3 or 500 metres by two times.
Friday:	Jog 30 minutes.
Saturday:	Development races over or under target distance.
Sunday:	Aerobic 60/90 minutes.

Continuation of Training and Racing

Monday:	Wind sprint 50 metres by 12/20.
Tuesday:	Easy fartlek or aerobic 60 minutes.
Wednesday:	Trial over-race distance (fast).
Thursday:	Fast relaxed striding 100 metres by six times.
Friday:	Jog 30 minutes.
Saturday:	Race or trial over half race distance.
Sunday:	Aerobic 60/90 minutes.

Monday:	Wind sprint 50 metres by 10/16.
Tuesday:	Trial 400/600/1,500 metres.
Wednesday:	Fast relaxed striding 100 metres by six times.
Thursday:	Jog 45 minutes.
Friday:	Jog 30 minutes.
Saturday:	The first important race
Sunday:	Jog 60/90 minutes or more.

The Marathon – You Can Do It

Many women run these days for fitness and health. Some are middle-aged, some are old, some are quite young. Few are concerned about being champions; most enjoy fun runs and the social interaction of being with people with a shared interest.

But they usually like to see their times improving. The schedules of aspiring champions are too tough for them; they need a programme that will enable them to race every one, two or three weeks without injury or loss of form.

Joan Ullyot, whose contributions to this book are gratefully acknowledged, was trained by me to run a marathon in 2:50 in her forties.

The following non-race week/race week schedule makes that possible, as long as the conditioning base is in place. It is important to intersperse long races with shorter ones, and to recover by merely jogging each day until back to normal.

Cross-country

	Non-race week
Monday:	Reps 1,500 metres by 300 or 800 metres by six times.
Tuesday:	Aerobic 60/90 minutes.
Wednesday:	Trial 2,000/3,000 metres.
Thursday:	Aerobic 60/90 minutes.
Friday:	Relaxed fast striding 100 metres by ten times.
Saturday:	Trial 2,000/3,000 metres.
Sunday:	Aerobic 90 minutes or more.

	Race week
Monday:	Wind sprint 100 metres by 6/10 times.
Tuesday:	Easy fartlek 45/60 minutes.
Wednesday:	Trial 1,600/2,400 metres.
Thursday:	Fast relaxed striding 100 metres by six times.
Friday:	Jog 30 minutes.
Saturday:	Race.
Sunday:	Aerobic 90 minutes or more.

Road Racing

Non-race week

Monday:	Reps, either 1,500 metres by 3 or 800 metres by six times.
Tuesday:	Aerobic 90 minutes.
Wednesday:	5,000 metres time trial.
Thursday:	Aerobic 60/90 minutes.
Friday:	Fast relaxed striding 100 metres by 6/10 times.
Saturday:	5,000 metres time trial.
Sunday:	Aerobic 90 minutes or more.

Race week

Monday:	Wind sprint 100 metres by 6/10 times.
Tuesday:	Easy fartlek 45/60 minutes.
Wednesday:	1,500 metres time trial.
Thursday:	Fast relaxed striding 100 metres by 4/6 times.
Friday:	Jog 30 minutes.
Saturday:	Race.
Sunday:	Aerobic 90 minutes or more.

Fun Run Schedule for Beginners

For six weeks

Monday:	Jog 15/30 minutes.
Tuesday:	Jog 30/60 minutes.
Wednesday:	Jog 15/45 minutes.
Thursday:	Jog 30/45 minutes.
Friday:	Rest or jog 30 minutes.
Saturday:	Jog 15/45 minutes.
Sunday:	Jog 30/60 minutes.

For four weeks

Monday:	Relaxed striding 100 metres by 4/6 times.
Tuesday:	Jog 30/60 minutes.
Wednesday:	Time trial 3,000 metres.
Thursday:	Jog 30/60 minutes.
Friday:	Rest or jog 30 minutes.
Saturday:	Time trial 5000 metres.
Sunday:	Jog 45/75 minutes.

For four weeks

Monday:	Relaxed striding 200 metres by 4/6 times.
Tuesday:	Jog 30/60 minutes.
Wednesday:	Time trial 3,000 metres.
Thursday:	Easy fartlek running 30/45 minutes.
Friday:	Rest or jog 30 minutes.
Saturday:	Time trial 5,000 metres.
Sunday:	Jog 60/90 minutes.

For four weeks

Monday:	Repetitions 800 metres by 2/4 times.
Tuesday:	Jog 30/60 minutes.
Wednesday:	Time trial 3,000 metres.
Thursday:	Easy fartlek running 30/45 minutes.
Friday:	Rest or jog 30 minutes.
Saturday:	Time trial 5,000 metres and 10,000 metres in alternate weeks.
Sunday:	Jog 60/90 minutes.

For two weeks

Monday:	Reps 1,500 metres by 2/3 times.
Tuesday:	Jog 30/60 minutes.
Wednesday:	Time trial 5,000 metres.
Thursday:	Fast relaxed running 100 metres by 4/8 times.
Friday:	Rest or jog 30 minutes.
Saturday:	1st week time trial 5,000 metres; second week time trial 10,000 metres.
Sunday:	Jog 60/90 minutes.

One week

Monday:	100 metres wind sprint every 200 metres by 6/8 times.
Tuesday:	Jog 45 minutes.
Wednesday:	Time trial 2,000 metres.
Thursday:	Fast relaxed running 100 metres by 4/6 times.
Friday:	Rest or jog 30 minutes.
Saturday:	Time trial 3,000 metres.
Sunday:	Jog 45/60 minutes.

One week

Monday:	Fast relaxed running 100 metres by 6/8 times.
Tuesday:	Time trial 1,000 metres.
Wednesday:	Jog 45 minutes.
Thursday:	Jog 30 minutes.
Friday:	Rest or jog 30 minutes.
Saturday:	Fun run.
Sunday:	Jog 45/60 minutes.

800 METRES

For as long a time as possible – at least 12 weeks

Monday: Aerobic running 30/60 minutes.
Tuesday: Aerobic 60/90 minutes.
Wednesday: Aerobic 30/60 minutes.
Thursday: Aerobic 60/90 minutes.
Friday: Aerobic 30/60 minutes.
Saturday: Aerobic 60 minutes.
Sunday: Aerobic 90 minutes or more.

Four weeks

Monday: Hill springing/bounding/steps running 30/60 minutes.
Tuesday: High knee lift exercise, long striding and running tall.
Wednesday: Hill springing/bounding/steps running 30/60 minutes.
Thursday: Leg speed 100 metres by 6/10 times.
Friday: Relaxed striding 200 metres by six times.
Saturday: Hill springing/bounding/steps running 30/60 minutes.
Sunday: Aerobic run 90 minutes or more.

One week

Monday: Reps 1,600 metres by three times.
Tuesday: Easy fartlek 45/60 minutes.
Wednesday: Repetitions 800 metres by six times.
Thursday: Fast relaxed running 100 metres by ten times.
Friday: Jog 30 minutes.
Saturday: Reps 1,000 metres by four times.
Sunday: Jog 30/60 minutes.

One week

Monday:	Reps 800 metres by six times.
Tuesday:	Easy fartlek 45/60 minutes.
Wednesday:	Reps 1,600 metres by three times.
Thursday:	Fast relaxed running 100 metres by ten times.
Friday:	Jog 30 minutes.
Saturday:	Reps 600 metres by six times.
Sunday:	Jog 90 minutes.

One week

Monday:	Reps 600 metres by six times.
Tuesday:	Easy fartlek 45/60 minutes.
Wednesday:	Reps 300 metres by three times fast.
Thursday:	Fast relaxed running 100 metres by ten times.
Friday:	Jog 30 minutes.
Saturday:	Reps 400 metres by 8/12 times.
Sunday:	Jog 90 minutes.

One week

Monday:	Reps 800 metres by six times.
Tuesday:	Easy fartlek 45/60 minutes.
Wednesday:	Reps 3,300 metres by three times fast.
Thursday:	Fast relaxed running 100 metres by ten times.
Friday:	Jog 30 minutes.
Saturday:	Reps 400 metres by 8/12 times.
Sunday:	Jog 90 minutes.

One week

Monday:	100 metres wind sprint every 200 metres by 6/10 times.
Tuesday:	Easy fartlek 45 minutes.
Wednesday:	Time trials 200 and 600 metres.
Thursday:	Fast relaxed running 100 metres by ten times.
Friday:	Jog 30 minutes.
Saturday:	Time trial 1,500 metres.
Sunday:	Jog 90 minutes.

One week

Monday:	100 metres wind sprint every 200 metres by 6/10 times.
Tuesday:	Easy fartlek 45 minutes.
Wednesday:	Time trials 200 and 600 metres.
Thursday:	Fast relaxed running 100 metres by ten times.
Friday:	Jog 30 minutes.
Saturday:	Time trial 800 metres.
Sunday:	Jog 90 minutes.

One week

Monday:	100 metres wind sprint every 200 metres by 6/10 times.
Tuesday:	Easy fartlek 45 minutes.
Wednesday:	Time trials 200 and 1,000 metres.
Thursday:	Fast relaxed running 100 metres by ten times.
Friday:	Jog 30 minutes.
Saturday:	Time trial 1,500 metres.
Sunday	Jog 60 minutes.

One week

Monday:	100 metres wind sprint every 200 metres by 6/10 times.
Tuesday:	Easy fartlek 45 minutes.
Wednesday:	Time trials 200 and 600 metres.
Thursday:	Fast relaxed running 100 metres by ten times.
Friday:	Jog 30 minutes.
Saturday:	Time trial 800 metres.
Sunday:	Jog 60 minutes.

One week

Monday:	45 metres wind sprint every 100 metres by 20 times.
Tuesday:	Easy fartlek 45 minutes.
Wednesday:	Time trial 800 metres.
Thursday:	Fast relaxed running 100 metres by ten times.
Friday:	Jog 30 minutes.
Saturday:	Time trial 600 metres.
Sunday:	Jog 60 minutes.

One week

Monday:	45 metres wind sprint every 100 metres by 12 times.
Tuesday:	Easy fartlek 30 minutes.
Wednesday:	Time trial 400 metres.
Thursday:	Fast relaxed running 100 metres by six times.
Friday:	Jog 30 minutes.
Saturday:	First important race.

1,500 Metres and 3,000 Metres

For as long as possible

Monday:	Aerobic 60 minutes.
Tuesday:	Aerobic 90 minutes.
Wednesday:	Aerobic 60 minutes.
Thursday:	Aerobic 105 minutes.
Friday:	Aerobic 60 minutes.
Saturday:	Aerobic 65 minutes.
Sunday:	Aerobic 120/150 minutes.

Four weeks

Monday:	Relaxed striding 300 metres by six times.
Tuesday:	Hill springing and bounding; steep hill/steps running 60 minutes.
Wednesday:	Sprint training.
Thursday:	Hill springing and bounding; steep hill/steps running 60 minutes.
Friday:	Jog 30 minutes.
Saturday:	Hill springing and bounding; steep hill/steps running 60 minutes.
Sunday:	Aerobic run 120/150 minutes.

One week

Monday:	Relaxed striding 300 metres by six times.
Tuesday:	Hill springing and bounding; steep hill/steps running 60 minutes.
Wednesday:	Sprint training.
Thursday:	Hill springing and bounding; steep hill/steps running 60 minutes.
Friday:	Jog 30 minutes.
Saturday:	Hill springing and bounding; steep hill/steps running 60 minutes.
Sunday:	Aerobic run 120/150 minutes.

One week

Monday: Relaxed striding 300 metres by six times.

Tuesday: Hill springing and bounding; steep hill/steps running 60 minutes.

Wednesday: Sprint training.

Thursday: Hill springing and bounding; steep hill/steps running 60 minutes.

Friday: Jog 30 minutes.

Saturday: Hill springing and bounding; steep hill/steps running 60 minutes.

Sunday: Aerobic run 120/150 minutes.

One week

Monday: Relaxed striding 300 metres by six times.

Tuesday: Hill springing and bounding; steep hill/steps running 60 minutes.

Wednesday: Sprint training.

Thursday: Hill springing and bounding; steep hill/steps running 60 minutes.

Friday: Jog 30 minutes.

Saturday: Hill springing and bounding; steep hill/steps running 60 minutes.

Sunday: Jog 120/150 minutes.

One week

Monday: Reps 800 metres by six times.

Tuesday: Easy fartlek 60 minutes.

Wednesday: Reps 300 metres by three times fast.

Thursday: Sprint training.

Friday: Jog 30 minutes.

Saturday: Reps 200 metres by ten times.

Sunday: Jog 120 minutes.

One week

Monday:	Reps 1,000 metres by four times.
Tuesday:	Easy fartlek 60 minutes.
Wednesday:	Reps 300 metres by three times.
Thursday:	Sprint training.
Friday:	Jog 30 minutes.
Saturday:	Reps 200 metres by ten times.
Sunday:	Jog 120 minutes.

One week

Monday:	Reps 1,000 metres by four times.
Tuesday:	Easy fartlek 60 minutes.
Wednesday:	Reps 300 metres by three times.
Thursday:	Sprint training.
Friday:	Jog 30 minutes.
Saturday:	Reps 400 metres by eight times.
Sunday:	Jog 120 minutes.

One week

Monday:	Time trial 3,000 metres.
Tuesday:	Reps 200 metres by 16 times.
Wednesday:	Sprint training.
Thursday:	Reps 300 metres by three times.
Friday:	Jog 30 minutes.
Saturday:	Reps 400 metres by eight times.
Sunday:	Jog 120 minutes.

One week

Monday:	Time trial 3,000 metres.
Tuesday:	Reps 200 metres by ten times.
Wednesday:	Sprint training.
Thursday:	Reps 300 metres by three times.
Friday:	Jog 30 minutes.
Saturday:	Reps 400 metres by eight times.
Sunday:	Jog 120 minutes.

One week

Monday:	100 metres wind sprint every 200 metres by 12 times.
Tuesday:	Easy fartlek 60 minutes.
Wednesday:	Time trials 200 and 600 metres.
Thursday:	Fast relaxed running 100 metres by ten times.
Friday:	Jog 30 minutes.
Saturday:	Time trial 3,000 metres.
Sunday:	Jog 90 minutes.

One week

Monday:	100 metres wind sprint every 200 metres by 12 times.
Tuesday:	Easy fartlek 60 minutes.
Wednesday:	Time trials 200 and 600 metres.
Thursday:	Fast relaxed running 100 metres by ten times.
Friday:	Jog 30 minutes.
Saturday:	Time trial 800 metres.
Sunday:	Jog 90 minutes.

One week

Monday:	100 metres wind sprint every 200 metres by ten times.
Tuesday:	Easy fartlek running 60 minutes.
Wednesday:	Time trials 200 metres and 1,000 metres.
Thursday:	Fast relaxed running 100 metres by ten times.
Friday:	Jog 30 minutes.
Saturday:	Time trial 3,000 metres.
Sunday:	Jog 90 minutes.

One week

Monday:	100 metres wind sprint every 200 metres by ten times.
Tuesday:	Easy fartlek 60 minutes.
Wednesday:	Time trials 200 metres and 600 metres.
Thursday:	Fast relaxed running 100 metres by ten times.
Friday:	Jog 30 minutes.
Saturday:	Time trial 1,500 metres.
Sunday:	Jog 90 minutes.

One week

Monday:	45 metres wind sprint every 100 metres by 20 times.
Tuesday:	Easy fartlek 45 minutes.
Wednesday:	Time trials 200 metres and 3,000 metres.
Thursday:	Fast relaxed running 100 metres by ten times.
Friday:	Jog 30 minutes.
Saturday:	Time trial 800 metres.
Sunday:	Jog 60 minutes.

One week

Monday:	45 metres wind sprint every 100 metres by 12 times.
Tuesday:	Easy fartlek 30 minutes.
Wednesday:	Time trial 800 metres.
Thursday:	Fast relaxed striding 100 metres by six times.
Friday:	Jog 30 minutes.
Saturday:	The 1,500 or 3,000 metres race.
Sunday:	Jog 90 minutes.

5,000 Metres

As long a time as possible

Monday:	Aerobic 30/60 minutes.
Tuesday:	Aerobic 60/90 minutes.
Wednesday:	Aerobic 30/60 minutes.
Thursday:	Aerobic 60/90 minutes.
Friday:	Aerobic 30/60 minutes.
Saturday:	Aerobic 60 minutes.
Sunday:	Aerobic 90/150 minutes.

Two weeks

Monday:	Easy fartlek 30/60 minutes.
Tuesday:	Aerobic 60/90 minutes.
Wednesday:	Easy fartlek 30/60 minutes.
Thursday:	Aerobic 60/90 minutes.
Friday:	Relaxed striding 200 metres by six times.
Saturday:	Aerobic 60 minutes.
Sunday:	Aerobic 90/150 minutes.

Four weeks

Monday:	Hill springing, bounding, steep hill/steps running 30/60 minutes.
Tuesday:	Aerobic 60/90 minutes.
Wednesday:	Hill springing, bounding, steep hill/steps running 30/60 minutes.
Thursday:	Easy fartlek 30/60 minutes.
Friday:	Relaxed striding 200 metres by six times.
Saturday:	Hill springing, bounding, steep hill/steps running 30/60 minutes.
Sunday:	Aerobic 90/120 minutes.

One week

Monday:	Reps 800 metres by six times.
Tuesday:	Easy fartlek 45/60 minutes.
Wednesday:	Time trial 5 kms.
Thursday:	Sprint training.
Friday:	Jog 30 minutes.
Saturday:	Time trial 400 metres by 8/12 times.
Sunday:	Jog 90/120 minutes.

One week

Monday:	Reps 1,500 metres by three times.
Tuesday:	Easy fartlek 45/60 minutes.
Wednesday:	Time trial 5 kms.
Thursday:	Sprint training.
Friday:	Jog 30 minutes.
Saturday:	Reps 200 metres by 8/12 times.
Sunday:	Jog 90/120 minutes.

One week

Monday:	Reps 1,000 metres by four times.
Tuesday:	Easy fartlek 45/60 minutes.
Wednesday:	Time trial 5 kms.
Thursday:	Sprint training.
Friday:	Jog 30 minutes.
Saturday:	Reps 400 metres by 8/12 times.
Sunday:	Jog 90/120 minutes.

One week

Monday:	Reps 800 metres by six times.
Tuesday:	Easy fartlek 45/60 minutes.
Wednesday:	Time trial 5 kms.
Thursday:	Fast relaxed running 100 metres by ten times.
Friday:	Jog 30 minutes.
Saturday:	Reps 200 metres by 8/15 times.
Sunday:	Jog 90/120 minutes.

One week

Monday:	100 metres wind sprint every 200 metres by 8/12 times.
Tuesday:	Easy fartlek 45/60 minutes.
Wednesday:	Time trials 200 and 800 metres.
Thursday:	Fast relaxed running 100 metres by ten times.
Friday:	Jog 30 minutes.
Saturday:	Time trial 3 kms.
Sunday:	Jog 60/90 minutes.

One week

Monday:	100 metres wind sprint every 200 metres by 8/12 times.
Tuesday:	Easy fartlek 45/60 minutes.
Wednesday:	Time trials 200 and 1000 metres.
Thursday:	Fast relaxed running 100 metres by ten times.
Friday:	Jog 30 minutes.
Saturday:	Time trial 3 kms.
Sunday:	Jog 60/90 minutes.

One week

Monday:	100 metres wind sprint every 200 metres by 8/12 times.
^Tuesday:	Easy fartlek 45 minutes.
Wednesday:	Time trials 200 and 800 metres.
Thursday:	Fast relaxed running 100 metres by ten times.
Friday:	Jog 30 minutes.
Saturday:	Time trial 10 kms.
Sunday:	Jog 60 minutes.

One week

Monday:	100 metres wind sprint every 200 metres by 8/12 times.
Tuesday:	Easy fartlek 45 minutes.
Wednesday:	Time trials 200 and 1,500 metres.
Thursday:	Fast relaxed running 100 metres by ten times.
Friday:	Jog 30 minutes.
Saturday:	Time trial 5 kms.
Sunday:	Jog 60 minutes.

One week

Monday:	45 metres wind sprint every 100 metres by 15/20 times.
Tuesday:	Easy fartlek 30/45 minutes.
Wednesday:	Time trial 5 kms.
Thursday:	Fast relaxed running 100 metres by ten times.
Friday:	Jog 30 minutes.
Saturday:	Time trial 1,500 metres.
Sunday:	Jog 60 minutes.

One week

Monday:	45 metres wind sprint every 100 metres by 12/16 times.
Tuesday:	Time trial 800 metres.
Wednesday:	Fast relaxed running 100 metres by six times.
Thursday:	Jog 45 minutes.
Friday:	Jog 30 minutes.
Saturday:	First important 5,000 metres race.
Sunday:	Rest

10,000 Metres

As long a time as possible

Monday:	Aerobic 60 minutes.
Tuesday:	Aerobic 60/90 minutes.
Wednesday:	Aerobic 60 minutes.
Thursday:	Aerobic 60/90 minutes.
Friday:	Aerobic 30 minutes.
Saturday:	Aerobic 60 minutes.
Sunday:	Aerobic 120 minutes.

Two weeks

Monday: Easy fartlek 60 minutes.
Tuesday: Aerobic 90 minutes.
Wednesday: Hill springing 45 minutes.
Thursday: Aerobic 90 minutes.
Friday: Relaxed striding 200 metres by six times.
Saturday: Aerobic 60 minutes.
Sunday: Aerobic 120 minutes.

Four weeks

Monday: Hill springing, bounding, steep hill or steps running 30/60 minutes.
Tuesday: Jog 90 minutes.
Wednesday: Hill springing, bounding, steep hill or steps running 30/60 minutes.
Thursday: Easy fartlek 60 minutes.
Friday: Relaxed striding 200 metres by six times.
Saturday: Hill springing, bounding, steep hill or steps running 30/60 minutes.
Sunday: Jog 90/120 minutes.

One week

Monday: Reps 800 metres by six times.
Tuesday: Jog 90 minutes.
Wednesday: Time trial 3,000 metres at 75 per cent effort.
Thursday: Easy fartlek 60 minutes.
Friday: Jog 30 minutes.
Saturday: Reps 400 metres by 12 times.
Sunday: Jog 90/120 minutes

One week

Monday:	Reps 1,500 metres by three times.
Tuesday:	Jog 90 minutes.
Wednesday:	Time trial 5,000 metres at 75 per cent effort.
Thursday:	Easy fartlek 60 minutes.
Friday:	Jog 30 minutes.
Saturday:	Reps 200 metres by 15 times.
Sunday:	Jog 90/120 minutes.

One week

Monday:	Reps 1,000 metres by four times.
Tuesday:	Jog 90 minutes.
Wednesday:	Time trial 3,000 metres at 75 per cent effort.
Thursday:	Easy fartlek 60 minutes.
Friday:	Jog 30 minutes.
Saturday:	Reps 400 metres by 12 times.
Sunday:	Jog 90/120 minutes

One week

Monday:	Reps 800 metres by six times.
Tuesday:	Jog 90 minutes.
Wednesday:	Time trial 1,500 metres.
Thursday:	Easy fartlek 60 minutes.
Friday:	Jog 30 minutes.
Saturday:	Time trial 3,000 metres.
Sunday:	Jog 90/120 minutes.

One week

Monday:	100 metres wind sprint every 200 metres by 12 times.
Tuesday:	Easy fartlek 60 minutes.
Wednesday:	Time trial 5,000 metres.
Thursday:	Fast relaxed running 100 metres by ten times.
Friday:	Jog 30 minutes.
Saturday:	Race 5,000 metres.
Sunday:	Jog 90 minutes.

One week

Monday:	100 metres wind sprint every 200 metres by 12 times.
Tuesday:	Easy fartlek 60 minutes.
Wednesday:	Time trial 3,000 metres.
Thursday:	Fast relaxed running 100 metres by ten times.
Friday:	Jog 30 minutes.
Saturday:	Race 10,000 metres.
Sunday:	Jog 90 minutes.

One week

Monday:	100 metres wind sprint every 200 metres by 12 times.
Tuesday:	Easy fartlek 60 minutes.
Wednesday:	Time trial 5,000 metres.
Thursday:	Fast relaxed running 100 metres by ten times.
Friday:	Jog 30 minutes.
Saturday:	Race 5,000 metres.
Sunday:	Jog 90 minutes.

One week

Monday:	100 metres wind sprint every 200 metres by 12 times.
Tuesday:	Easy fartlek 60 minutes.
Wednesday:	Time trial 1,500 metres.
Thursday:	Fast relaxed running 100 metres by ten times.
Friday:	Jog 30 minutes.
Saturday:	Race 10,000 metres.
Sunday:	Jog 90 minutes.

One week

Monday:	45 metres wind sprint every 100 metres by 20 times.
Tuesday:	Easy fartlek 45 minutes.
Wednesday:	Time trial 1,500 metres.
Thursday:	Fast relaxed running 100 metres by ten times.
Friday:	Jog 30 minutes.
Saturday:	Race 5,000 metres.
Sunday:	Jog 60 minutes.

One week

Monday:	45 metres wind sprint every 100 metres by 16 times.
Tuesday:	Time trial 800 metres.
Wednesday:	Fast relaxed running 100 metres by six times.
Thursday:	Jog 30 minutes.
Friday:	Jog 30 minutes.
Saturday:	First important 10,000 metres race.
Sunday:	Rest.

Marathon

Women, again as a general rule, have more subcutaneous fat in the muscles than men and this seems to give them an advantage in real endurance. The fat is a natural storehouse of energy they can use before running into deficit.

In Copenhagen in 1971 two doctors specialising in cardiology put on a 100 km fun run which drew about a hundred starters. I had not seen an ultra before so I was keenly interested in the outcome, and intrigued to see that, at the end of the race, most of the men were lying down and relaxing and the women were still standing up talking.

They still do not run as fast as men, of course, because they do not have the same muscle power – probably about 30% to 40% less – although there are the inevitable exceptions of weak men and strong women. I do not think women's oxygen uptake level is as high as men's, which means they do not have the cardio-respiratory efficiency to run marathons as fast as men. They cannot generate and sustain power, drive and speed as economically as men, but there is no reason why, sooner or later, a woman cannot cover the distance in 2:18. They have the same limitations I predicted more than 30 years ago about men – that, at this stage of human evolution, it is not physically possible for a man to run under two hours for a marathon. We are still stuck around 2:05.

However, women's marathon times have improved faster than men's because, until a couple of decades ago, few women ran the distance and they did not train properly. Now, many women train as hard as men and their times are coming down as fast as their confidence is rising.

It is worth noting here that New Zealand has produced many world-class women distance runners – Anne Audain, Mary O'Connor, Lorraine Moller, Alison Deed, Toni Hodgkinson, Heather Thomson are some of them – but there are many more fine performers who have not raced abroad. They emerged from clubs they joined when they were 13 or 14, clubs which gave them regular training and competition in all seasons.

The first requirement if you want to run a marathon for a reasonable result is an application of intelligence. Give yourself plenty of time for development, take the long view. Some people are credited with running exceptionally fast marathons on as little as 32 km of training a week, but many of these times are far from authentic. They have been run on downhill courses, and with tail wind assistance, on courses with start and finish points many miles apart.

However, anyone with no physical or health limitations could walk a marathon if they had to. Or they could walk and run it. But to run it all the way without stopping, and without undue stress, requires a reasonable weekly training mileage, possibly close to 80-100 km for several months.

This does not mean haphazard training; it needs a schedule which takes into consideration your basic fitness and running background. The schedule is a guide to the sequence of all the elements you need. All you have to do is fit it into the time you have available before your target race – and then get running.

The novice marathoner should tackle shorter distances first but this is not imperative. Condition yourself by training for a period of time each day rather than running set mileages. This usually gives better results, and keeps off the pressure that can arise when your time for a set distance one day may not be as fast as the time you set earlier.

Allow three days a week for long runs – what you consider long depends on your level of fitness, but the aim should be 90 minutes on two days and two hours or more on one day. This extra-long run can be increased every four or five weeks to take you nearer the time you will spend on your feet when you run the marathon itself.

The in-between days are used for runs up to 60 minutes over varying terrain to strengthen the legs and general condition, or for rest. If your legs get unduly tired ignore the schedule and lighten the training for a few days until you have recovered and can run again in reasonable comfort. The risk in pushing yourself when you feel tired is that you could suffer muscle breakdown which will waste all your previous effort.

The best results come when you train to a reasonably tired state, knowing as you finish that the training could have been harder. Keep in mind that you can never run too slowly but you can run too fast.

About three months of long aerobic running of this kind achieves the desired minimum conditioning base. During that third month add a day or two of easy fartlek to ready yourself for the faster training involved in the next phase, but keep that constant balance between long days and short days.

Always think about your running technique and speed as you train. Use hilly terrain or steps to help leg strength and flexibility. This can be done in a secondary training session each day; warm-up and then bound a few easy hills, run some stadium steps or a steep hill, or do a little sprinting on a gentle slope to work the ankles. You do not need a lot, just enough to make you feel the workout.

After the conditioning period of at least three months, four to six weeks can be used to concentrate on hill-type training to add resistance to your leg muscles and develop muscle fibres. Two or three workouts a week, from 15 to 60 minutes depending on how you feel, is enough. It is better to underdo than overdo.

The other days, use for steady running, striding or easy fartlek. How your legs feel dictates what you do. Try relaxed downhill striding on gentle slopes.

The third phase requires some anaerobic running for three days with the rest being taken relatively easily. If you do reps, use the longer distances – over 800 metres six times or 1,500 metres three times – because you are likely to have more muscular viscosity than athletes training for shorter distances, and fast short reps could cause injury. The tempo must be governed by how you feel and less is better than more.

Five weeks away from the marathon you can ease your effort slightly but, about four weeks out, a trial simulating actual race conditions can be run. Anything from 32 km to the full distance works. It will give you a good indication of the result you can expect, although you will not be as fresh for the trial as you will be for the big race itself. The trial will help you to check your pace judgement. Any mistake you make will be in the front of your mind a month later. It will also enable you to check your reactions to food and drink before and during the race.

But the greatest benefit will be a sharp improvement in your racing fitness. You will retain this new plane by keeping all further training relatively easy and resisting the temptation to run too much in the final week. It is too late by then to add anything to your state of preparedness but you could risk lowering it.

Maintain normal balanced meals leading up to the marathon. In the two days before eat up to 250 grams extra honey or sugars. Do not eat in the three hours before the start. If you have a breakfast, make it light – preferably cereals, honey and toast with tea or coffee.

Do not wear new shoes. They should be comfortably broken in. Make sure you put them on correctly, forcing the heels into the back of the shoes and lacing firmly, but not tightly, to prevent foot slippage inside the shoe which could cause blisters.

Do not run around too much before you start. Save your energy. Stretch and loosen a little by all means, then use the early part of the race as your warm-up. Many modern marathons have such large fields anyway, that, except for the "guns" who shoot away to the front, most runners cannot get into their planned racing paces for quite a distance.

Stay relaxed. Whatever the runners around you are doing, ignore them. Do your own planned thing. Do not let yourself get panicked by runners going past you but stick firmly to the effort that suits you. The dividends will be paid later. Far too many inexperienced runners – and quite a few experienced ones – overdo the early stage effort because they latch on to others and try to foot it with them, and then hit the wall.

Prepare electrolyte drinks for a hot day but make the mixture weaker than the label suggests and add some honey. Do not take salt tablets. Drink water and electrolytes throughout the race; and if you have not got a proper drinking vessel stop to drink to avoid gulping air.

Keep your body wet by squeezing sponges over your head, even dump a bucket of water over yourself. It is insurance against dehydration and high body temperature.

Resist any temptation to surge during the race. It uses energy you will need for the closing stages.
    Do not use anti-perspirants.

Beginners Marathon

	Four weeks
Monday:	Jog 30/45 minutes.
Tuesday:	Jog 45/60 minutes.
Wednesday:	Jog 30/45 minutes.
Thursday:	Jog 45/60 minutes.
Friday:	Jog 30 minutes.
Saturday:	Jog 45 minutes.
Sunday:	Jog 60 minutes.

Two weeks

Monday:	Aerobic 30/45 minutes.
Tuesday:	Jog 60/75 minutes
Wednesday:	Aerobic 30/45 minutes.
Thursday:	Jog 60/75 minutes.
Friday:	Jog 30 minutes.
Saturday:	Aerobic 30/45 minutes.
Sunday:	Jog 60/90 minutes.

Four weeks

Monday:	Easy fartlek 30/45 minutes.
Tuesday:	Aerobic 45/75 minutes.
Wednesday:	Easy fartlek 30/45 minutes.
Thursday:	Aerobic 45/75 minutes.
Friday:	Relaxed striding 150 metres by 4/6 times.
Saturday:	Easy fartlek 45/60 minutes.
Sunday:	Aerobic 60/120 minutes.

Four weeks

Monday:	Hill springing/bounding, steep hill/steps running 30/45 minutes.
Tuesday:	Aerobic 45/75 minutes.
Wednesday:	Easy fartlek 30/45 minutes.
Thursday:	Hill springing/bounding, steep hill/steps running 30/45 minutes.
Friday:	Relaxed striding 200 metres by 4/6 times.
Saturday:	Hill springing/bounding, steep hill/steps running 30 minutes.
Sunday:	Aerobic 60/120 minutes.

One week

Monday:	Reps 800 metres by 2/4 times.
Tuesday:	Aerobic 45/75 minutes.
Wednesday:	Time trial 3,000 metres.
Thursday:	Aerobic 45/75 minutes.
Friday:	Relaxed striding 200 metres by 4/6 times.
Saturday:	Time trial 5,000 metres.
Sunday:	Aerobic 90/120 minutes.

One week

Monday:	Reps 1,000 metres by 2/3 times.
Tuesday:	Aerobic 60/90 minutes.
Wednesday:	Time trial 3,000 metres.
Thursday:	Aerobic 60/75 minutes.
Friday:	Relaxed striding 200 metres by 4/6 times.
Saturday:	Time trial 10,000 metres.
Sunday:	Aerobic 90/120 minutes

One week

Monday:	Reps 1,500 metres by 2/3 times.
Tuesday:	Aerobic 60/90 minutes.
Wednesday:	Time trial 5,000 metres.
Thursday:	Aerobic 60/90 minutes.
Friday:	Relaxed striding 200 metres by 4/6 times.
Saturday:	Time trial 5,000 metres.
Sunday:	Aerobic 90/120 minutes.

One week

Monday:	Reps 800 metres by 3/5 times.
Tuesday:	Aerobic 60/90 minutes.
Wednesday:	Time trial 3,000 metres.
Thursday:	Easy fartlek 45 minutes.
Friday:	Relaxed striding 200 metres by 4/6 times.
Saturday:	Time trial 10,000 metres.
Sunday:	Aerobic 90/120 minutes.

One week

Monday:	100 metres wind sprint every 200 metres by 6/8 times.
Tuesday:	Jog 60/90 minutes.
Wednesday:	Time trial 5,000 metres.
Thursday:	Jog 60/90 minutes.
Friday:	High knee lift exercise 100 metres by six times.
Saturday:	Time trial 3,000 metres.
Sunday:	Jog 60/90 minutes.

One week

Monday:	100 metres wind sprint every 200 metres by six times.
Tuesday:	Jog 60 minutes.
Wednesday:	Time trial 2,000 metres.
Thursday:	Jog 45 minutes.
Friday:	Jog 30 minutes.
Saturday:	Time trial 35 kms – fast!.
Sunday:	Jog 30/45 minutes.

One week

Sunday:	Jog 45/60 minutes.
Monday:	Jog 45/60 minutes.
Tuesday:	Relaxed striding 200 metres by six times.
Wednesday:	Time trial 3,000 metres.
Thursday:	Easy fartlek 30 minutes.
Friday:	Jog 30 minutes.
Saturday:	Time trial 3,000 metres.
Sunday:	Jog 120 minutes.

One week

Monday:	100 metres wind sprint every 200 metres by 6/8 times.
Tuesday:	Jog 60/90 minutes.
Wednesday:	Time trial 3,000 metres.
Thursday:	Jog 60/90 minutes.
Friday:	Jog 30 minutes.
Saturday:	Time trial 10,000 metres.
Sunday:	Jog 90/120 minutes.

One week

Monday:	100 metres wind sprint every 200 metres by 6/8 times.
Tuesday:	Jog 60/90 minutes.
Wednesday:	Time trial 5,000 metres.
Thursday:	Easy fartlek 30/45 minutes.
Friday:	Jog 30 minutes.
Saturday:	Time trial 3,000 metres.
Sunday:	Jog 45/60 minutes.

One week

Monday:	Fast relaxed running 100 metres by six times.
Tuesday:	Time trial 2,000 metres.
Wednesday:	Jog 45 minutes.
Thursday:	Jog 30 minutes.
Friday:	Jog 30 minutes.
Saturday:	Marathon race.
Sunday:	Jog easily for one week.

Marathon

For as long as possible (12 weeks or more)

Monday:	Aerobic 60 minutes.
Tuesday:	Aerobic 90 minutes.
Wednesday:	Aerobic 60 minutes.
Thursday:	Aerobic 90 minutes.
Friday:	Aerobic 60 minutes.
Saturday:	Aerobic 60 minutes.
Sunday:	Aerobic 120 minutes or more.

Four weeks

Monday:	Hill springing/bounding, steep hill/steps running 45/60 minutes.
Tuesday:	Aerobic 90 minutes.
Wednesday:	Hill springing/bounding, steep hill/steps running 45/60 minutes.
Thursday:	Easy fartlek 60 minutes.
Friday:	Relaxed striding 200 metres by six times.
Saturday:	Hill springing/bounding, steep hill/steps running 45/60 minutes.
Sunday:	Aerobic 120 minutes.

One week

Monday:	Reps 800 metres by six times.
Tuesday:	Aerobic 90 minutes.
Wednesday:	Time trial 5,000 metres,.
Thursday:	Aerobic 90 minutes.
Friday:	Relaxed striding 200 metres by six times.
Saturday:	Time trial 10,000 metres at 75 per cent effort.
Sunday:	Aerobic 120 minutes.

One week

Monday:	Reps 1,000 metres by four times.
Tuesday:	Aerobic 90 minutes.
Wednesday:	Time trial 5,000 metres.
Thursday:	Aerobic 90 minutes.
Friday:	Relaxed striding 200 metres by six times.
Saturday:	Time trial 10,000 metres at 75 per cent effort.
Sunday:	Aerobic 120 minutes or more.

One week

Monday:	Reps 1,500 metres by three times.
Tuesday:	Aerobic 90 minutes.
Wednesday:	Time trial 5,000 metres.
Thursday:	Aerobic 90 minutes.
Friday:	Relaxed striding 200 metres by six times.
Saturday:	Time trial 5,000 metres.
Sunday:	Aerobic 120 minutes or more.

One week

Monday:	Reps 800 metres by six times.
Tuesday:	Aerobic 90 minutes.
Wednesday:	Time trial 3,000 metres.
Thursday:	Aerobic 90 minutes.
Friday:	Relaxed striding 200 metres by six times.
Saturday:	Time trial 10,000 metres.
Sunday:	Aerobic 120 minutes or more.

One week

Monday:	100 metres wind sprint every 200 metres by 10/12 times.
Tuesday:	Jog 90 minutes.
Wednesday:	Time trial 5,000 metres.
Thursday:	Jog 90 minutes.
Friday:	Fast relaxed running 100 metres by six times.
Saturday:	Time trial 5,000 metres.
Sunday:	Jog 90 minutes.

One week

Monday:	100 metres wind sprint every 200 metres by 10/12 times.
Tuesday:	Jog 90 minutes.
Wednesday:	Time trial 3,000 metres.
Thursday:	Jog 60 minutes.
Friday:	Jog 30 minutes.
Saturday:	Time trial 35 kms – fast!
Sunday:	Jog 60 minutes.

One week

Monday:	Jog 60 minutes.
Tuesday:	Relaxed striding 200 metres by six times.
Wednesday:	Time trial 5,000 metres
Thursday:	Jog 90 minutes.
Friday:	Jog 30 minutes.
Saturday:	Time trial 3,000 metres.
Sunday:	Jog 120 minutes.

One week

Monday:	100 metres wind sprint every 200 metres by 10/12 times.
Tuesday:	Jog 90 minutes.
Wednesday:	Time trial 3,000 metres.
Thursday:	Jog 90 minutes.
Friday:	Jog 30 minutes.
Saturday:	10,000 metres time trial.
Sunday:	Jog 120 minutes.

One week

Monday:	100 metres wind sprint every 200 metres by ten times.
Tuesday:	Jog 90 minutes.
Wednesday:	Time trial 5,000 metres.
Thursday:	Easy fartlek 45 minutes.
Friday:	Jog 30 minutes.
Saturday:	Time trial 5,000 metres.
Sunday:	Jog 60 minutes.

One week

Monday:	Fast relaxed running 100 metres by six times.
Tuesday:	Time trial 2,000 metres.
Wednesday:	Jog 45 minutes.
Thursday:	Jog 30 minutes.
Friday:	Jog 30 minutes.
Saturday:	Marathon race.
Sunday:	Jog 60 minutes and then jog easily for one week.

20 Postscript – The Legend Strides on

Arthur Lydiard is 81 now and the power of his persuasion is undimmed. If anything it is stronger than ever. Hundreds of thousands of words have been written in the past four decades about the remarkable success of the Lydiard system of endurance training. Tens of thousands of runners and joggers have adopted – sometimes adapted but never improved – his methods.

Just about every time a middle or distance runner hits the finishing tape he or she has got there by reproducing the Lydiard system in their own bodies. Just about every middle and distance record which is set these days has the touch of the master somewhere in the achievement.

In 1984, Jeff Galloway in his book *Galloway's Book of Running,* wrote:
"I was running before it (running) caught on in America. Then, in the late '60s, I began to see a trickle of other runners out on the roads I once ran alone. By the early '70s there were more and, now, millions are out running regularly. It seemed to have been a natural evolution, but in retrospect we can pinpoint a few key people who helped propel running into the revolution we now see: three teachers – Arthur Lydiard, Bill Bowerman and Dr Kenneth Cooper; and three runners – Amby Burfott, Frank Shorter and Bill Rodgers. These six were catalysts, reflecting and magnifying the spirit of the times. They were at the right places, at the right time, with the right inspiration for the new outlook that was crucial to the birth of fitness running.

"Lydiard invented jogging ... transformed the public image of running from an intense, tedious, painful activity into a social, civilised component of the active New Zealand lifestyle. The credit of (his athletes') Olympic medals in 1960 gave Lydiard a platform from which to reach millions. He got them out of their chairs and onto the roads ... and the underground running movement began."

Galloway recalls that Bowerman, in New Zealand with his University of Oregon track team, became a jogger under the guidance of Lydiard and took the principle home to the United States. Cooper, discovering, as Bowerman had done with Lydiard, that he was dangerously unfit, developed his system of aerobics. The distance running achievements of Burfoot, who broke the Finnish and Japanese stranglehold on the famous Boston marathon, and Shorter and Rodgers, added the final inspiration.

In 1997, John Hawley, director of the High Performance Laboratory at the Sports Science Institute of South Africa, made this comment in his internet column:

"I doubt if any coach will ever have more impact on the training practices of endurance athletes than Arthur Lydiard. He revolutionised training with regard to the volume of work he thought an athlete should perform in their conditioning phase. His programmes were simple, based on a consistent, thorough and direct application of hard work. Lots of it.

'Unfortunately, many athletes and coaches have misinterpreted his conditioning phase as merely 160 kms a week of long slow distance running. This was not his strategy. Neither was it a rigid requirement. His athletes were regularly running 160 kms a week at their best aerobic effort but, in addition, were supplementing their training with easier sessions, often totalling up to 250 kms a week! He advocated running year round and pointed out that any athlete training six days a week could not hope to beat one who trained every day.

An equally important contribution was Lydiard's concept of periodisation. He knew an athlete could not train hard and perform well simultaneously. He mixed different types of conditioning – the long mileage, the hill work, the speed work, the sharpening and freshening – so his runners arrived at the start line at their peak."

And in September 1998, the *Irish Runner* magazine carried this tribute from contributing writer Dick Hooper:

"Raheny Library first opened in 1972. Big, spacious, quiet. Good sports section. Great selection of athletics' books. All three of them. *No Bugles, No Drums* by Peter Snell and Garth Gilmour, *The Unforgiving Minute* by Ron Clarke and *Run To The Top* by Arthur Lydiard and Garth Gilmour. Our bible.

Jim Aherne, John Maher and I competed for these books like it was the last lap of a track race. Two weeks first, then renewed for another two before the other guy spotted you.

We read Snell and Clarke because we wanted to be like them. Lydiard was different. He was the one who told us how to get there. The training, the sacrifices. And his book full of powerful New Zealanders dressed in the all black with the silver fern. God please reincarnate me and bring me back to earth as a New Zealander in Arthur Lydiard's camp.

That vest. The ultimate performance enhancement drug. I remember in Christmas 1972 getting a black vest and black shorts, training in St Anne's Park and imagining myself to be like Peter Snell. Kiwi runners were always so exciting ....

Arthur Lydiard was responsible for all that. If Frank Shorter invented running in America then it was Lydiard who planted the harvest worldwide. The ultimate guru.

I first ran 100 miles in a week when I was 16 because Arthur Lydiard recommended it. Ah, they were the days when boys were men. No heart monitors or orthotics, no Nike Air or Irish Runner. Runners were like a minority church group. The disciples of Arthur Lydiard.

Lydiard was a pioneer in running and coaching terms. Everything he coached, he had tried himself. He experimented with every day training, twice a day training, things that were alien to the nature at the time. He reasoned that many athletes had speed but that few had endurance. He worked out the art of peaking. His was a philosophy based on the work ethic."

After so many years as a lone voice, it is heart-warming to Lydiard today to have so many joining in his anthem.

Garth Gilmour
Auckland
November 1998

Our English Programme

Jozef Sneyers
Soccer Training
An Annual Programme
ISBN 1-84126-017-7
c. DM 34 ,-/SFr 31,60/ÖS 248,-
£ 12.95/US$ 19.95
Austr.$ 29.95/Can$ 29.95

Bischops/Gerards
Soccer
Warming-up and Cooling down
ISBN 1-84126-014-2
c. DM 24,80/SFr 23,-/ÖS 181,-
£ 8.95/US$ 14.95
Austr.$24.95/Can$ 20.95

Bischops/Gerards
Soccer
One-On-One
ISBN 1-84126-013-4
c. DM 24,80/SFr 23,-/ÖS 181,-
£ 8.95/US$ 14.95
Austr.$24.95/Can$ 20.95

Gerhard Frank
Soccer
Creative Training
ISBN 1-84126-015-0
c. DM 24,80/SFr 23,-/ÖS 181,-
£ 8.95/US$ 14.95
Austr.$24.95/Can$ 20.95

Erich Kollath
Soccer
Techniques & Tactics
ISBN 1-84126-016-9
c. DM 24,80/SFr 23,-/ÖS 181,-
£ 8.95/US$ 14.95
Austr.$24.95/Can$ 20.95

Gerhard Frank
Soccer Training Programmes
ISBN 3-89124-556-4
DM 29,80/SFr 27,70/ÖS 218,-
£ 12.95/US$ 17.95
Austr.$ 29.95/Can$ 25.95

Bischops/Gerards
Junior Soccer:
A Manual for Coaches
ISBN 1-84126-000-2
DM 29,80/SFr 27,70/ÖS 218,-
£ 12.95/US$ 17.95
Austr.$ 29.95/Can$ 25.95

Bischops/Gerards
Coaching Tips for Children's Soccer
ISBN 3-89124-529-7
DM 14,80/SFr 14,40/ÖS 108,-
£ 5.95/US$ 8.95
Austr.$ 14.95/Can$ 12.95

Pieter/Heijmans
Scientific Coaching for Olympic Taekwondo
ISBN 3-89124-389-8
DM 29,80/SFr 27,70/ÖS 218,-
£ 12.95/US$ 17.95
Austr.$ 29.95/Can$ 25.95

Rudolf Jakhel
Modern Sports Karate
ISBN 3-89124-428-2
DM 29,80/SFr 27,70/ ÖS 218,-
£ 12.95/US$ 17.95
Austr.$ 29.95/Can$ 25.95

Ilona E. Gerling
Teaching Children's Gymnastics
ISBN 3-89124-549-1
DM 29,80/SFr 27,70/ÖS 218,-
£ 12.95/US $ 17.95
Austr.$ 29.95/Can$ 25.95

Thomas Kaltenbrunner
Contact Improvisation
ISBN 3-89124-485-1
DM 29,80/SFr 27,70/ÖS 218,-
£ 12.95/US$ 17.95
Austr.$ 29.95/Can$ 25.95

Dörte Wessel-Therhorn
Jazz Dance Training
ISBN 3-89124-499-1
DM 29,80/SFr 27,70/ÖS 218,-
£ 12.95/US$ 17.95
Austr.$ 29.95/Can$ 25.95

Bergmann/Butz
Adventure Sports – Big Foot
ISBN 3-89124-497-5
DM 34 ,-/SFr 31,60/ÖS 248,-
£ 14.95/US$ 19.95
Austr.$ 29.95/Can$ 29.95

Münch/ Mund
Straight Golf
ISBN 3-89124-503-3
DM 34,-/SFr 31,60/ÖS 248,-
£ 12.95/US$ 19.95
Austr.$ 29.95/Can$ 25.95

● **Publication date: Fall 1999/Spring 2000**

MEYER
&MEYER
SPORT

Our English Programme

Hömberg/Papageorgiou
Handbook for Beach-Volleyball

ISBN 3-89124-322-7
DM 38,-/SFr 35,30/ÖS 278,-
£ 17.95/US$ 29.-
Austr.$ 37.95/Can$ 39.95

Neumann/Pfützner/ Berbalk
Successful Endurance Training ●

ISBN 1-84126-004-5
DM 34 ,-/SFr 31,60/ÖS 248,-
£ 12.95/US$ 17.95
Austr.$ 29.95/Can$ 29.95

Richard Schönborn
Advanced Techniques for Competitive Tennis

ISBN 3-89124-534-3
DM 38.-/SFr 35,30/ÖS 278,-
£ 17.95/US $ 29.-
Austr. $ 37.95/Can $ 39.95

Papageorgiou/Spitzley
Volleyball:
A Handbook for Coaches and Players

ISBN 1-84126-005-3
DM 34 ,-/SFr 31,60/ÖS 248,-
£ 14.95/US$ 19.95
Austr.$ 29.95/Can$ 29.95

Kuno Hottenrott
The Complete Guide to Duathlon Training

ISBN 3-89124-530-0
DM 34 ,-/SFr 31,60/ÖS 248,-
£ 14.95/ US$ 19.95
Austr.$ 29.95/Can$ 29.95

Lutz Steinhöfel
Training Exercises for Competitive Tennis

ISBN 3-89124-464-9
DM 29,80/SFr 27,70/ÖS 218,-
£12.95/US$ 17.95
Austr.$ 29.95/Can$ 25.95

Georg Neumann
Nutrition in Sport ●

ISBN 1-84126-003-7
c. DM 34 ,-/SFr 31,60/ ÖS 248,-
£ 12.95/US$ 17.95
Austr.$ 29.95/Can$ 29.95

Hermann Aschwer
The Complete Guide to Triathlon Training

ISBN 3-89124-515-7
DM 34 ,-/SFr 31,60/ÖS 248,-
£ 12.95/US$ 19.95
Austr.$ 29.95/Can$ 29.95

Dieter Koschel
Allround Fitness
The Beginner's Guide

ISBN 1-84126-011-8
DM 24,80/SFr 23,-/ÖS 181,-
£ 9.95/US $ 14.95
Austr.$ 24.95/Can$ 20.95

Bös/Saam
Walking
Fitness and Health through Everyday Activity

ISBN 1-84126-001-0
DM 14,80/SFr 14,40/ÖS 108,-
£ 5.95/US$ 8.95
Austr.$ 14.95/Can$ 12.95

Achim Schmidt
Handbook of Competitive Cycling

ISBN 3-89124-509-2
DM 34 ,-/SFr 31,60/ÖS 248,-
£ 12.95/US$ 19.95
Austr.$ 29.95/Can$ 29.95

Bettina M. Jasper
Train your Brain

Mental and Physical Fitness

ISBN 3-89124-531-9
DM 29,80/SFr 27,70/ÖS 218,-
£12.95/US$ 17.95
Austr.$ 29.95/Can$ 25.95

Petracic/Röttgermann/Traenckner
Successful Running

ISBN 1-84126-006-1
DM 24,80/SFr 23,-/ÖS 181,-
£ 9.95/US$ 14.95
Austr.$ 24.95/Can$ 20.95

Achim Schmidt
Mountainbike Training

ISBN 1-84126-007-X
DM 29,80/SFr 27,70/ÖS 218,-
£ 12.95/US$ 17.95
Austr.$ 29.95/Can$ 25.95

Uwe Rheker
Integration through Games and Sports

ISBN 1-84126-012-6
DM 29,80/SFr 27,70/ÖS 218,-
£ 12.95/US $ 17.95
Austr.$ 29.95/Can $ 25.95

MEYER & MEYER SPORT

e-mail: verlag@meyer-meyer-sports.com • **Please order by:** www.meyer-meyer-sports.com

Please order our English catalogue!

**MEYER
&MEYER
SPORT**

Meyer & Meyer Sport • Von-Coels-Str. 390 • D-52080 Aachen • Fax: 0049241/9 58 10 10

Lydiard's Coaching Books

Lydiard/Gilmour
Distance Training for Women Athletes

ISBN 1-84126-002-9
DM 24,80/SFr 23,-/ÖS 181,-
£ 9.95/US$ 14.95
Austr.$ 24.95/Can$ 20.95

Lydiard Gilmour
Distance Training for Masters ●

ISBN 1-84126-018-5
c. DM 29,80/SFr 27,70/ÖS 218,-
£ 12.95/US$ 17.95
Austr.$ 29.95/Can$ 25.95

Lydiard/Gilmour
Distance Training for Young Athletes

ISBN 3-89124-533-5
DM 29,80/SFr 27,70/ÖS 218,-
£ 12.95/US$ 17.95
Austr.$ 29.95/Can$ 25.95

Arthur Lydiard
Running to the Top

ISBN 3-89124-440-1
DM 29,80/SFr 27,70/ÖS 218,-
£ 12.95/US$ 17.95
Austr.$ 29.95/Can$ 25.95

Arthur Lydiard revolutionised the training of middle and long distance runners in the 1960s. Since then his methods have contributed to the success of countless athletes around the world, including four time Olympic gold medalist and world record setter Lasse Viren of Finland.

Do you want to improve your training? – Let Lydiard be your personal coach!
For US$ 240,-/year only Lydiard offers you personal training plans and advice.

For more information turn to

www.lydiard.com

or

www.meyer-meyer-sports.com

MEYER & MEYER SPORT

Order worldwide: Great Britain/Ireland: Windsor Books International Fax: 0044/ 18 65 361 133
Canada: Prologue Fax: 001-450 434 2627
Australia/New Zealand: Bookwise International Fax: 00618/ 8268/ 8704
USA: Partners Book Distributing, Inc. Fax: 001-517-694-0617